FOR THE

oblivious/indifferent/skeptical

HUSBAND

Everything a Man needs to know about

Network Marketing, Essential Oils, and Young Living

(without having to ask his wife)

What's in this Book?

I Dare you to Read this Section and not Laugh

Congratulations! You made it farther in the book than many men would have. Seriously, great job! Keep going . . .

Answer to your first question: This book is about Network Marketing, essential oils, and understanding your wife's Young Living business. Unlike many books about these subjects, it is written for men, not women; it has humour, not hype.

Answer to your second question: You should care because this book addresses the most common questions and complaints men have about Network Marketing and essential oils, and, guess what? In spite of what your wife keeps telling you, not all of your opinions are wrong (about these topics at least).

To answer your third question: Yes, you can read this book while in the bathroom or while watching NASCAR – and yes, of course you can look up during the crashes – in fact, I insist on it.

This is the book I wish someone would have given me when my wife started with Young Living. It is informative but still entertaining – it has a fishing story, a hunting example, numerous sports analogies, and some car references – what else could a guy want in a book about Network Marketing and essential oils?

What this book is NOT

This book is not a sales pitch. This book was not written to convince you to get involved in Network Marketing. It wasn't written to persuade you to use essential oils or to sway you to Young Living. I don't care if you get involved in Network Marketing (it's not for everyone) or if you join your wife in building a Young Living business. I just want you to understand all of it so you can make the decisions that are best for you.

WARNING!

Before you read any further, I must warn you that although there is an excellent chance that a woman bought this book, it is not meant for women, it is meant for guys.

Some wives might read it, and most ladies will learn from it, but make no mistake, this book was written for dudes.

If you are a woman, and you choose to read this book, please don't send me a nasty email because you didn't get the sports references, you are morally opposed to hunting, or the bathroom humour offended you. And please, please, please, ma'am, stop reading now if you are the type who would lose her mind if a man ever implied (insisted?) that not only does he understand the pain of childbirth, he has experienced something 100 times worse, okay?

Guys, now that it is just us, you can undo that top button and let out your gut. Here we go . . .

What I assume about you:

- You did not buy this book.
- You do not want to read this book.
- You think the content of this book is probably a bunch of garbage.

You probably also fit into one or more of these categories:

1) You are indifferent about your wife's oil business,

2) You don't know much about Network Marketing and/or essential oils, or

3) You think Network Marketing and/or essential oils are scams.

If you aren't sure if any of these categories apply to you, let me help you with some examples:

You are likely in category one, the *Indifferent Husband,* if this scenario sounds familiar:

Your wife says to you, "Honey, I am having a few friends over for a class tonight to learn about essential oils."

Without looking up, your response is one of the following:

- "Will there be food left over?"
- "If I stay downstairs, do I have to put on pants?"
- Silence. It was late in the fourth quarter of the game you were watching so, well . . . you know.

The key to identifying if you are in this first category is that your interest in her business can be summed up in the question, *how will this affect me?* Your support for her business is inversely related to how much it puts you out. In other words [read this next part with a caveman voice]: *Me have to put on pants, me no like business; Me get leftover cheeseball, me luuuv business!*

There is a sub-group of the Indifferent Husband category: the *Oblivious Husband.* You are in this sub-group if the first time you found out that your wife was in a Network Marketing organization was when she handed you this book. If this describes you, it is safe to say that you are in this category and that this book will help you immensely (but, c'mon man, no wonder she is always choked at you!).

The second category of husband is the *Average Guy* (aka, *the comedian*). You may be in this category, if you have asked any of the following:

- "Sponsor? You mean like in Alcoholics Anonymous?"
- "Is this a pyramid scheme? Are you going to go to jail? If you go to jail, who will make me pudding?"

- "I overheard you on the phone saying your OGV was high this month, you aren't having another baby, are you? I told you to be careful!"

Men in this category are the easiest to spot when they are in a co-ed group: if the guys are laughing their heads off while the women are getting more and more angry, you've got yourself a posse of *average guys*.

This category also has a sub-group: the *Supportive Husband*. If you are in this sub-group, you think of all the same hilarious remarks as the average husband but you are smart enough not to say them out loud.

You are in category three, the *Skeptical Husband*, if you have heard yourself say to your wife (or if your neighbors have heard you yelling) one or more of the following:

- "What reeks?"
- "Get that stuff off my feet!"
- "How much did you blow on these?"

Most of these comments are questions or exclamations expressed at a volume much louder than normal conversation (except, of course, the whiny ones, which are mumbled under your breath).

If you wanted to follow other skeptical husbands on Twitter, you would probably do searches like #snakeoil, #wasteofmoney, or #Networkmarketingscam (if this last one doesn't connect you with like-minded individuals, try #MLMscam).

At this point, most guys have identified themselves into one of the three groups above . . . and then promptly forgotten which category they were in. Doesn't matter – just read the rest of the book 'cuz ya know your wife is going to ask – wha-tish! (how do you type a whipping noise?)

> *If you are overdue for a trip to the bathroom and/or can't wait to read more of this book, try swallowing a tablespoon of olive oil*

To estimate how long it will take you to trudge through this book and get back to playing Candy Crush on the throne, you have probably already thumbed through it to see how many pages there are and if there are any pictures. I'll give you an idea. Many guys use this book as a bathroom reader, so how long it will take you to read it depends on your intake of things like veggies and red meat – if it takes you less than three days or more than 3 weeks, you may want to see a doctor. Enjoy!

Part 1: Network Marketing

In this section, you will learn the basics of Network Marketing. This includes its structure, history, legality, income opportunity, and much, much more – read carefully if you want a fighting chance against your wife.

If you already know all there is to know about Network Marketing, you should read these chapters even more carefully than the newbie. It's because you are acting like such an arrogant know-it-all that your wife bought you this book in the first place!

1. What is Network Marketing?

Read this sentence slowly so you don't miss it:

> Network Marketing is people *marketing* products or services to their *networks*.

Profound, eh?

Any time you share about a product or service you like, you are Network Marketing. Tell a buddy how great the latest *Expendables* movie is – Network Marketing. Go to the new steak house in town and post a picture of the 32 ounce hunk of beef on your plate – Network Marketing. And, the next day when you tweet how great your plumber is for unclogging your toilet – also Network Marketing.

Marketing:

The process of interesting people in a product or service

Think back to how you discovered your current mechanic, doctor, accountant, attorney, realtor, babysitter, barber, and maybe even your wife – probably through Network Marketing. There is a good chance that you are in the profession you are in and you have the employer you do because of Network Marketing. You are both the provider and recipient of Network Marketing almost every day – it's just that no one has been paying you for it.

Why not?

While all businesses covet your favourable reviews, they rarely reward you for them. Unlike those freeloading non-Network Marketing companies, Network Marketing companies compensate you for recommending their products to your friends and family.

Network Marketing is based on two underlying philosophies:

1. It is better to have many salesmen that each sell a little than it is to have a few salesmen that each try to sell a lot. This philosophy is similar to the recent trend from venture capitalists toward crowdfunding. And,
2. A prospective buyer is much more likely to do business with someone they know, like, and trust.

Network Marketing/Multi-Level Companies have existed since the 1940s

These two philosophies affect how a company is structured and, more importantly, they influence how companies compensate their people. Below, I compare Network Marketing with another marketing model that has often been used in the past 200 years, retail sales. Because it is more familiar, I will begin with retail.

Retail

Companies that utilize the retail marketing model usually operate from fixed location stores. Common examples of retail stores are Walmart, Bank of America, McDonalds, Cineplex, and your local Ford dealership. To market their products, these companies mainly rely on paid advertisements (TV, radio, internet, magazines, billboards, etc.), paid endorsements, and paid sponsorships.

When you recommend the products sold through retail businesses, they do not usually pay you for your complimentary testimonial. Instead, for marketing and advertising, they pay ad companies and celebrity endorsers (more on this in Chapter 11). As a rule, retail companies only pay employees for sales.

Rather than an hourly wage, retail companies sometimes pay their employees a commission on their sales. This compensation plan can be referred to as *single-level* marketing because payment is made to one level: the person who made the sale. Compare the retail model to Network Marketing.

Network Marketing

Network Marketing is a business model that utilizes word-of-mouth advertising to expand sales volume. Rather than spending money on retail stores and mass advertising, companies rely on one-on-one presentations ("coffee shop meetings"), home parties, or portable booths (trade shows) to market their goods.

In Network Marketing, salespeople are not employees of the company. Instead, they are *independent distributors*. In addition to earning money from their own sales, Network Marketers may recruit additional distributors and earn commissions and bonuses from their sales. Because distributors can be paid for sales beyond their own explains why Network Marketing is often referred to as *multi-level* marketing (MLM).

Employee vs Independent Distributor

There are advantages to being an employee and advantages to being an independent distributor. Below are three advantages of each:

Advantages of being an employee:

1. Defined hours/responsibilities
2. Defined hourly wage/salary
3. Company benefits

Advantages of being an independent distributor:

1. Be your own boss (set your own hours, live and work where you want, etc.)
2. Greater income potential
3. Generous tax incentives

Take a moment and review the advantages of being an employee and the advantages of being an independent distributor. What type of person would each business model attract?

People who tend towards clear directions, security, and predictability are suited to be employees. People who seek freedom, autonomy, and wealth are attracted to the entrepreneurial aspects of being an independent distributor.

I want to make a few things clear:

- A person drawn to the benefits of entrepreneurialism is not inherently better than one drawn to being an employee (or vice versa). They are just two different mindsets.
- If your wife has no interest in being an entrepreneur, she can just be a customer of the products – no big deal. Succeeding as an entrepreneur requires commitment.
- Just because your wife has never been an entrepreneur does not mean she cannot succeed – skill development is often one of Network Marketing's greatest benefits.

Comparing the lists also demonstrates why many people (maybe your wife) struggle when they start with Network Marketing – it can sometimes be difficult to make the shift from employee to entrepreneur. The great thing about your wife being her own boss is there is no one telling her what she has to do, so she does not have to do anything. The bad part about doing nothing is that nothing is likely what she will be paid.

An employee trades time for money.

A Network Marketing entrepreneur trades time to build a business.

Network Marketers – like all entrepreneurs – focus more on building a business than on receiving a regular paycheque. These people are not (necessarily) insane, they just hope that at some point the business will pay mucho money. The upside of this strategy is that the payoff could be enormous. The downside is that there is no set timetable for this payday (or even a guarantee that payday will ever come).

The implications of the employee mindset compared with the mindset of an entrepreneur are enormous. If your wife is getting frustrated in her Network Marketing business, you can likely trace it back to an employee mindset.

A Network Marketing organization (your wife's downline) is a business entity. It can be sold, transferred, or willed.

In reality, most people love the ideas of unlimited income potential and being their own boss, but they hate the idea of giving up the security of a regular paycheque. Combine this desire for stability with the time it often takes to shift to an entrepreneurial mindset and build a significant income, and you see why nearly all Network Marketers begin part-time.

What determines if a company sells retail or through Network Marketing?

The marketing model a company uses is *not* determined by the product or service they sell – it is about how they pay to have their product marketed. In the following examples, the first company sells retail and the second uses Network Marketing:

- L'Oréal and Mary Kay (both sell cosmetics)
- MetLife and Primerica (life insurance)
- Rubbermaid and Tupperware (food storage containers)

Which method a company uses is not right or wrong, it simply indicates the philosophies of the companies and how they think their product will best get into the market.

When you think of a Network Marketing company, if you envision a Mickey Mouse operation where a couple of fat guys with plumber butts are sitting on upside-down pails in their garage scooping weight loss powder into Ziplocs, you will be shocked by what you read in the next chapter.

2. How Big is the Network Marketing Industry?

Guys want a big TV, a big steak, a big gun, a big bank account, a big truck, a big mug of beer, and big biceps. If I really thought about it, I could probably list even more things they want big. With a few notable exceptions, you name it, guys probably want it big.

Even though we have seen some very large blue chip companies go belly-up in the last few years, when it comes to how most men assess legitimate businesses, size matters – and bigger is better.

"I don't know how to put this . . . but . . .
I'm kind of a big deal."

Ron Burgundy in *The Anchorman*

Network Marketing Revenue

Is Network Marketing big? Check out these stats for 2016:

- U.S. Network Marketing sales: $35 billion
- Global Network Marketing sales: $200 billion
- The top 70 Network Marketing companies each earned more than $200 million

Some of the largest Network Marketing companies (with 2016 sales) are:

1st: Amway ($8.8 Billion)
2nd: Avon ($5.7 B)
5th: Mary Kay ($3.5 B)
10th: Tupperware ($2.2 B)
22nd: Young Living ($1.0 B)

For the average Joe Six-Pack working paycheque to paycheque, these numbers are tough to grasp. To help put them in perspective, compare these figures with the yearly revenue of a few professional sports teams:

- Dallas Cowboys ($700 Million)
- New York Yankees ($500 M)
- Toronto Maple Leafs ($186 M)
- Golden State Warriors ($170 M)

Many expect that Young Living will soon reach $1.5 billion in yearly sales* – nearly the same revenue as the four teams above combined [*just prior to publication, Young Living announced it had, in fact, surpassed $1.5B in 2017].

How many people are involved in Network Marketing?

In the United States, there are approximately 20 million people involved in over 1000 Network Marketing companies. Of these 20 million, about 5 million people service a customer base while 15 million just use products.

In Canada, the proportions are nearly identical to the U.S.: there are about 700,000 Network Marketers selling nearly $1 billion worth of goods and services.

In the United States:

- 74% of Network Marketers are female;

- One in six households has someone involved in Network Marketing;

- Nearly three in 10 people involved in Network Marketing are Millennials;

- People involved in Network Marketing have higher average incomes and more education than the average American

Like it or hate it, Network Marketing is kind of a big deal. Now, let's explore how it works so the next time you fight with your wife about it, you can catch her off guard by actually knowing what you are talking about . . .

3. The Principles of Network Marketing

Network Marketing compensation plans are set up based on the three activities needed to build a Network Marketing business:

1) Use the product,

2) Share the product/opportunity, and

3) Teach others to do #1 and #2.

Compare these three steps to a commission car salesman:

A salesman will usually drive the brand of car he is selling, and he is obviously trying to sell cars off the lot; so the first two premises are similar to Network Marketing. The difference lies in the third: Education.

Network Marketing companies not only want distributors to use and sell products; they want distributors to *teach* their customers (downline) to share the products with more potential customers. To encourage education, companies set up their compensation plans to reward distributors for their personal sales *as well as* the sales of their downline.

Is providing a financial incentive to sponsors for teaching recruits an effective strategy for ensuring a good education? Hmmm, I wonder . . .

Picture one of your kid's school teachers (or, if you have no clue what your kid's teacher looks like, imagine one of your old teachers). What do you think would happen to the quality of education that teacher would provide if he/she was paid a 3% commission on every dollar his/her students earned *over the course of their entire lives*?

Do you think it would affect the teacher's enthusiasm? His/her willingness to help? His/her attitude toward professional development?   Do you think that teacher would be more committed to the success of your child?   To the success of *every* child?

Network Marketing companies believe that teachers (sponsors) will do their best work when the compensation of the teacher largely depends on the success of their students (their downline).

Now that you understand the principles behind Network Marketing compensation plans, I will provide a more detailed breakdown of how your wife is paid and reveal the secret to making big money in this industry.

4. The Nuts and Bolts of Network Marketing

Network Marketing uses a combination of several marketing strategies with which you are already familiar.

It is a customer loyalty/referral program on steroids (not just baseball player steroids either, I'm talkin' professional wrestler steroids). What do I mean by that? I'll give you a real-world example:

Where I buy gas, I received a Customer Loyalty Card. The card was free (easy online form) and entitles me to 7 cents off for every litre of gas I buy at this station (for those of you who don't do metric, it works out to about 25 cents off/gallon). Companies often use this type of preferred customer incentive to retain your business – especially if they have competitors who offer a very similar product.

Loyalty Program benefits are based on *your* purchases. Besides at the gas station, you might receive discounted prices, free products, or even cash back on your purchases at your local grocery store, bakery, movie theatre, pet store, car wash, coffee shop, sub shop, and other retail outlets. Even McDonalds just finished a *buy 7 coffees, get one free* promotion. Loyalty programs are very common, and you are likely already signed up for at least a couple (just check your wallet for faded business cards with stamps).

Besides loyalty programs, a few companies offer *referral programs*. If you refer a friend to your realtor, lawyer, barber, or car salesman, you may get cash, a gift card, or a fruit basket as his or her way of saying thank you. Companies that use referral rewards are often local, self-employed professionals and/or salesmen for big-ticket items.

The thank you gifts for referring a new customer to these companies are one-time gestures – don't expect a basket of oranges to arrive at your door every time your buddy gets his hair cut. Ongoing rewards, on the other hand, are the steroids of Network Marketing.

In addition to loyalty rewards on her own sales, you know that new customer your wife just enrolled? Your wife will not only receive a referral bonus, she will earn a commission cheque for everything that person ever buys. What about all the new customers that person brings in? Your wife receives lifetime commissions on what *they* buy as well. And, when all those people bring in new customers, guess what? Your wife earns many, many commissions. How many levels this goes on for will vary, but you can see the potential of *Multi-Level* Marketing – commissions are paid indefinitely on multiple levels of customers.

Nearly anyone can get bigger by lifting weights, but when someone lifts weights *and* takes steroids, they get HUGE. Steroids are to weight lifting what commissions on your downline's sales are to Network Marketing (all this without the hair loss and kidney damage).

Why the Network Marketing Model works – company perspective

From the perspective of the company, Network Marketing works economically because they:

1. Save on the purchase and maintenance of brick and mortar locations.
2. Do not have to pay wages/benefits to (many) employees.
3. Drastically reduce advertising costs.

4. Reduce risk. Distributors are paid only after a sale is made.
5. Rely on independent distributors to provide education for new customers.
6. Charge distributors for much of the ongoing presentation/training/education costs (sample products, books, conventions, etc.).

This list is not comprehensive, but it gives you a good idea of why companies choose the Network Marketing model.

Downside of Network Marketing

I don't think you want me to expand on the whole list, but point #5 is worth exploring because it can be a shortcoming of the Network Marketing system.

Since the sales force is comprised of independent distributors (not employees), and because all training is optional and paid for by the distributor, it is very difficult for a Network Marketing company to oversee/control/standardize/mandate the training of its distributors. This variance in distributor knowledge, skills, and actions can lead to false claims, exaggerated promises, and unhappy customers.

Your wife wants to avoid making these mistakes. It is one thing if the salesman at Best Buy misrepresents something to a customer off the street, it is quite another when your wife hoodwinks your mom. Not cool.

If your wife likes to share about the oils and/or is planning to build a Network Marketing business, I highly recommend she take advantage of both company training as well as generic Network Marketing skills training. In the meantime, pay close attention to Chapter 10: *Will we Lose all our Friends?*

Why the Network Marketing Model works – distributor perspective

You have seen some of the advantages for a company to use a Network Marketing model, but how does it benefit independent distributors like your wife? From her perspective, Network Marketing works because she is eligible to receive the following financial benefits:

1. Discounts on purchases for personal use.
2. Free products.
3. Credit every month (e.g. 20% of purchase applied as credit for future order).
4. Paid percentage of downline orders.
5. Free trips, free prizes, and cash bonuses.
6. Wholesale products that can be resold at retail prices.
7. Tax savings

The above benefits can range anywhere from saving a few bucks on her oils to earning tens of thousands of dollars every month.

Helpful hint: When your wife helps someone sign up and make a first purchase, she may get excited about receiving a bonus, but this is *not* how she will make big money. This is *not* how she will make big money. Again? This is *not* how she will make big money.

> *"Many people don't realize that multi-level marketing companies are successful because they help people satisfy a number of important human needs, including feeling significant, having connections, learning something new, and making a difference. I have heard people in network marketing say again and again, 'I'm doing this because I'm meeting amazing people ... making so many connections ... and I feel so good about myself.'"*
>
> Daria M. Brezinski Ph.D

The secret(s) to earning big dough in Network Marketing:

One-time sales and enrollment bonuses are awesome, but in Network Marketing, your wife will earn the big bucks by:

1) Downline members getting on autoship (Young Living calls this Essential Rewards or E.R.), and,

2) Teaching her downline how to build teams (that do not require your wife).

Your wife may be tempted to focus on the short-term benefits, but the payoff is in the long-run. This will make more sense to you after reading Chapter 12.

In the meantime, #7 is something that can help put money in your pocket from day one. Tax saving is an enormous and often overlooked benefit that you must understand. In fact, after reading the following chapter, the next argument you have with your wife about Network Marketing might be because you realize you have been paying too much in taxes and you are angry with her for not starting her business sooner.

5. Tax Breaks

OK, I do not have a degree in accounting, but I do have one in economics, so I will start there (and do not take any of this as tax advice, consult a professional, blah, blah, blah*).

[*I have been informed that what I meant by "blah, blah, blah" was that nothing in this book should be considered tax or legal advice. I do not give tax or legal advice. All materials in this book are for informational purposes only and not to be taken as tax, legal, or accounting advice. For questions relating to taxes, talk to an accountant or a lawyer, or anyone but me.]

Economics is largely the study of incentives . . . investigating why people do what they do, and examining how different incentives influence behaviour. Allow me to illustrate with a completely hypothetical example . . .

Suppose that your 14 year old son's bedroom has fallen into less than pristine condition. It could be described as a pig sty – assuming the pig has just stopped caring. What incentives could you use to alter his behaviour?

You could yell at him. The incentives for him to clean up his room would be so you shut up and stop threatening him.

You could post a picture of his room, spamming his favourite social media sites with images of his SpongeBob underwear prominently displayed (make a contest out of it: best caption wins). This would likely provide him with sufficient incentive to clean his room to avoid further embarrassment (as well as plenty of incentive for retribution, I would not try this one).

If you are like me, though, you would most likely go with a financial incentive: you agree to pay him $10 a week for keeping his room clean. You are using money to provide an *incentive* to change his behaviour . . . this is basic economics.

Just as you might entice your son to get him to do his part in keeping your home suitable for human life, governments want to encourage their citizens to contribute to society.

Small Businesses are Big Business

In the U.S. [Forbes, 2012]:

- 28 million small businesses

- Two-thirds of new jobs came from small businesses

- Over half of the working population worked for a small business,

- 75% of businesses were non-employer (single person business like your wife's)

- Non-employer businesses had revenue of approximately one trillion dollars

- 52% of small businesses were home-based

While big corporations often get the headlines, small businesses drive the economies of most democratic countries. Governments (who want a thriving economy), therefore, want to encourage entrepreneurship. How? The same way you motivated your son to get off his butt: incentives. Primarily, *tax* incentives.

"You would have to be brain dead not to have a home-based business."

Sandy Botkin, CPA, tax lawyer, and former IRS legal specialist

Pretty much anything your wife spends on her Network Marketing business toward the goal of turning a profit may be deducted (written off) to lower her tax bill. This includes expenses like product giveaways, trade show fees, advertising, travel, and training programs.

Additionally, if she has a home office/work area, she may be able to deduct a portion of household expenses including water, power, gas, rent, mortgage interest, internet, phone, computer, and insurance. According to experienced home-based business accountant, Sandy Botkin, this could amount to $500 or more back in your pocket every month *from the day your wife starts business building.*

In the U.S., the IRS has provided further incentive to operate a business from home; home office expenses can now be calculated with a simplified method. See https://www.irs.gov/publications/p587#en_ US_2016_publink1000283

For now, this is what you need to know: If your wife is legitimately trying to build a Network Marketing business, governments want to help. For more information, talk to an accountant who specializes in home based businesses (tip: if an accountant does not have a home-based business of his/her own, you probably want to find one that does – no sense hiring a brain-dead accountant). You may be able to write off many expenses and pay less in taxes. This is money in your pocket – don't miss out.

This overview of legal tax incentives is the perfect segue (yes, that is how you spell segway, who knew?) into some other common concerns about the legality of Network Marketing. We will begin with the twin terrors: Ponzi and pyramid schemes . . .

6. Is Network Marketing a Ponzi Scheme?

Have you ever been having an argument and your opponent says something so stupid that you suddenly realize that they don't have a clue what they are talking about? Well, even if you haven't had this experience, your wife probably has . . . many times. If you have ever called Network Marketing a Ponzi scheme, you don't understand Network Marketing and/or you don't know what a Ponzi scheme is. Let me help you so, in the future, you can accurately criticize your wife and not sound like an ill-informed parrot.

First, what is the difference between a Ponzi scheme and a pyramid scheme?

Ponzi vs Pyramid

In a Ponzi scheme, swindlers mislead investors into thinking they will earn substantial returns from an investment. Unbeknownst to participants, however, any supposed investment gains are not coming from investments. Instead, payouts are actually coming from money provided by new investors.

By comparison, in a pyramid scheme participants are aware that they are earning money by finding new participants, and they willingly become part of the scheme.

Put simply, Ponzi schemes have the illusion of investment returns, while pyramid schemes are based on recruitment and (often) the illusion of product sales.

If either of these definitions applies to Network Marketing, it is clearly pyramids, but more about those pointy buggers later. First, just to make sure the accusation is put to rest forever, let's examine Ponzi schemes more closely.

Ponzi Schemes

Named for Italian Charles Ponzi, a Ponzi scheme is a con in which people are enticed by the promise of generous returns to give money towards a supposedly legitimate investment. In reality, however, their money simply goes to the architect of the scam. This ringleader then pays out just enough money to keep previous investors satisfied and confident in the system. His hope is that by keeping them happy, most will not ask for their money back (at least until new investors can be found to pay the original investors).

The charade continues until:

a) The ringleader suddenly skips town and you don't hear about him again until they find his body floating in the river, or

b) The amount of income from new investments does not cover the amount owed to previous investors. At this point, the ringleader will usually attempt to borrow money to cover his obligations (think bailout). When he can no longer scrape together enough funds, the ringleader's sons turn him in to the cops (ala Bernie Madoff).

In 1920s' Boston, Charles Ponzi duped investors out of $20 Million in a postage stamp scam that "robbed Peter to pay Paul"

From 1985 until 2008, investment advisor and former NASDAQ chairman, Bernie Madoff's Ponzi scheme cost investors an estimated $64 Billion

Obviously, Network Marketing has no resemblance to a Ponzi scheme, so save yourself the embarrassment and don't ever bring that one up with your wife.

Of course, this thing has to be a scam of some kind, right? So what do you do now? If you are like most guys, you will go to the grand-daddy of all oppositions to Network Marketing, the dreaded *pyramid scheme* objection (shudder) . . .

7. Is Network Marketing an Illegal Pyramid Scheme?

As predictable as the reaction when a doctor taps a guy's knee with a mallet, upon hearing the words *Network Marketing,* men automatically respond, "Network Marketing . . . is this one of those pyramid schemes?"

This question is so common, half of you guys probably skipped right to this chapter. If you did jump ahead, that's fine, I won't tell your wife, but make sure you go back and read Chapter 5 at some point – it could save you big bucks.

Back to those cursed 3-D triangles. Because so many people are concerned about sinister pyramid schemes, I will provide four – count them, four answers for your consideration: the short answer, the dictionary answer, the Hollywood answer, and finally, the legal answer.

Question: Are Network Companies illegal pyramid schemes?

1. Short answer: Roughly 99.75% of the time the answer is *no.* Historically, about one out of every 400 companies that promoted themselves as Network Marketing companies have been illegal pyramid schemes. More about these rubes and rogues in #4.

2. Dictionary answer: I get a kick out of this loaded question. It is always called a pyramid *scheme.* Why not a pyramid *compensation plan* or pyramid *structure*? It is never even referred to as a pyramid *scam.* Always a pyramid *scheme.* It reminds me of the word *succulent.* Is anything besides shrimp ever referred to as succulent? I digress.

By definition, a scheme is just a *plan*; it is not necessarily devious. You could have a *scheme* to build a house and use a colour *scheme* to decorate it. You could also say that Bill Belichick had a *scheme*

31

to help the Patriots' defense . . . whoa, bad example! Moving along . . .

3. Hollywood answer: If you have seen the classic Christmas movie, *Miracle on 34th Street*, you will understand how easy it is to show that Network Marketing is a legitimate business model. The story is a little different, but the logic is the same.

"There aren't going to be any damned permits. How do you get a permit to do a damned illegal thing?"

Dr. Leonard 'Bones' McCoy,
Star Trek III: Search for Spock

SPOILER ALERT (if you can have a spoiler from a movie made in 1947): In the Christmas classic, *Miracle on 34th Street*, the white bearded and jolly Kris Kringle claims to be the real Santa Claus. The case ends up in court. Kringle's lawyer produces bags and bags of letters addressed to Santa Claus that the U.S. Postal Service had delivered to Kringle. The judge pronounces that if the United States government deems Kringle to be Santa Claus, then he must legally be Santa Claus – case dismissed.

What . . . in the . . . world, you ask, does this have to do with Network Marketing?

As noted in Chapter 5, the IRS (U.S) and CRA (Canada) both encourage people to operate home-based businesses. This includes tax deductions for your wife's business as an independent distributor for a Network Marketing company.

If Network Marketing was illegal, the IRS and CRA would not allow business write-offs against earnings from Network Marketing companies. Now you understand why you never saw Walter (*Breaking Bad*) try to deduct his second cell phone expense from his meth earnings on his taxes – his wife was a bookkeeper, she knew that wouldn't fly. Summary:

- Tax agencies *do not* allow deductions from *illegally* earned income.

- Tax agencies *do* allow deductions from Network Marketers.

- Network Marketing *must be* legal.

4. Legal answer: A business model is determined to be an illegal pyramid scheme if the primary focus of the business is recruitment, and not the sales of goods or services. For example: *join our program by sending ten dollars to the top person on the list; you will then move to the top of the list, and five people will then each send you ten dollars.* Money is changing hands but there are no goods or services of value involved (I say "of value" because, for a while in the '80s, some shysters claimed that the envelope in which the money was sent constituted a product – nice try).

IMPORTANT: A compensation plan that rewards recruiting *without a significant focus on a product or service* is an illegal pyramid scheme (heads up! There will be a quiz on this later).

In 1979, the US Federal Trade Commission (FTC) ruled that Amway was a LEGAL Network Marketing company and NOT an illegal pyramid scheme for four reasons:

1) Distributors were not paid to recruit people,

2) Distributors were not required to buy a large stock of inventory,

3) Distributors were required to maintain retail sales, and

4) The company accepted returns of excess inventory from distributors.

Of the thousands of Network Marketing companies that have existed in the past several decades, a handful have been prosecuted for being pyramid schemes. The list of companies that shut down "voluntarily" (prior to court ruling) or by decree include:

- BurnLounge (2004-2007). Online music.
- Fortune Hi-Tech Marketing (2001-2013). Mobile phones, satellite dishes, home security etc.
- PrimeBuy Network (1999-2001). Wholesale products with PrimeBuy label.
- 2Xtreme Performance International/USAsurance Group/Akahi (1996-2001). Nutritional supplements.

As you can see, authorities discovered and shut down these shady companies relatively quickly. The primary reason they were deemed illegal pyramid schemes? Product sales were secondary to recruitment.

While I do not mean to belittle the money people lost because of the unscrupulous behavior of the execs at Burnlounge, et al., let's put it into perspective. The total amount involved in these MLM scams was pocket change compared to the amount people lost because of the fraudulent/unethical actions of executives at billion dollar companies like AIG, Citibank, Worldcom, Enron, Bear Stearns, Lehman Brothers, and Goldman Sachs. In fact, the amount lost to Network Marketing companies was a fraction of the amount paid *as bonuses* to the CEOs of these blue chips.

In 2008, financial services company, Merrill Lynch reported a $27 billion dollar loss and was awarded a government bailout of approximately $10 billion.

$3.6 billion of which was paid out to company executives

But hey, if someone is stealing *your* money, any amount matters, right?

To determine if the company your wife is involved with is legal, start with the compensation plan. Your wife should be paid commissions and bonuses based primarily on the products sold by her and her organization (her downline).

Companies are permitted to provide one-time bonuses to distributors for recruiting a new customer provided the new customer does not simply "sign up," but actually purchases a legit product. This is no different from a referral bonus as outlined in Chapter 4.

Some of your wife's income will be commissions from sales to the people she personally enrolled. Since she earns no set wages from her company, this is the same as a 100% commission salesman.

The majority of your wife's income, however, will come from earning a percentage of her downline's sales volume. This is comparable to a Sales Manager who is paid a percentage of what his sales team sells in a month. Like it does for a Sales Manager, this type of compensation plan is designed to encourage your wife not only to sell product, but, more importantly, to train sales people and to build teams.

Now that you have seen the criteria for differentiating between a legal Network Marketing company and an illegal pyramid scheme, we will dive even deeper.

When guys accuse Network Marketing companies of being "one of those pyramid schemes," some are not so much referring to the legality of the business model, but rather to the belief that the people at the bottom work like dogs while the few people at the top make all the money. The following two chapters will provide with some enlightening facts about pyramids that may shock you and cause you to re-evaluate the entire Network Marketing industry . . .

8. Pyramids: Sad but True Facts

We have concluded that Network Marketing is clearly legal, but it does have a pyramid structure. So, why in the world would your wife want to be a part of a system where those at the bottom make so little compared to those at the top? Why would anybody?

Consider the following statistics. Who would want to be involved in these pyramids?

Organization 1:

-   The wealth of the top 160 people is the same as the wealth of the remaining *145,000* people; and
-   The top 20 earners are worth more than the bottom 50% combined.

How would you feel about your wife signing up with these guys?

Not so good? Maybe you'll like the next one better.

Organization 2:

Organization 2 has 20 times more people than Organization 1. In this juggernaut,

-   The top 20% of earners hold 85% of wealth while bottom 40% holds only .3%; and,
-   The top eight earners are wealthier than bottom 50%.

Aside from the privileged few at the top, who in their right mind would ever participate in this obviously inequitable system? Not you, that's for sure! And it had better not be your wife, right?

What are the names of these diabolical wedge-shaped organizations that exploit the masses for the sake of a few?

Before I reveal the names, let me ask you, if it turns out that your wife's company is either of these pyramid organizations, will you "encourage" her to quit, or just let her continue on working to make someone else rich?

Ready? Here are their names . . .

Organization 1 represents a little upstart deal we call the *United States of America*. In the US, the wealthiest 160,000 households enjoy the same wealth as the remaining 145,000,000 (yes, 145 *million*) households.

If you are an American, you can blame the one percenters, you can blame the Federal Reserve, you can blame the bleeding-heart Democrats, or you can blame greedy Republicans (for the record, the wealth inequity has exploded in the 40 years leading up to these stats. During that time, the party in power was almost even – 18 years Democrat and 22 years Republican). Blame who you want, the facts remain.

"Wait a minute," you say, "I do not live in the US; I am not a part of their elitist economy." Maybe not, but I can guarantee you are a part of Organization 2 – the one that has even greater disparity – the planet Earth.

You read that correctly, the wealthiest *eight* individuals in the world are worth the same as the poorest *3.8 billion* people. Eight.

Wealth: The value of possessions a person owns at any given moment.

Income: How much money a person earns in a given period of time

---

The above numbers demonstrate a pyramid-shaped distribution of wealth, what about income?

If you are concerned that your wife should not do Network Marketing because "the people at the top make all the money," here is an enlightening quiz:

If your wife worked for the average Fortune 500 company, how many days would she have to work to earn as much money as the CEO earns in a day?

What's your guess?

Would you estimate it would take her five days to earn what the CEO earns in a day?

Ten days?

Ninety days?

Well, assuming your wife remained healthy, and assuming there were no bothersome labour laws requiring things like time off, stat. holidays, or vacation time; studies indicate that to earn as much as her CEO does in *one* day, your wife would have to work at least *380 straight days*.

Just for snickers, I decided to test this finding. I looked for a company near the middle of the Fortune 500 list that is in an industry similar to Young Living. I found retail cosmetics giant Estée Lauder (number 253 out of 500).

A quick search revealed that Estée Lauder CEO, Fabrizio Freda, earned 47.7 million dollars in 2016. During that same time, the average Estée Lauder beauty consultant pulled in about 27 grand. For my calculations, I assumed the CEO and the beauty consultant work the same number of days in a year.

How many days would she have to work?

Put it this way: Suppose they both started work on Jan 1, 2017. Freda worked just the one day and then hit the beach. In order to earn as much as Freda earned that day, his employee, the beauty consultant, would have to work *every day* until Hallowe'en . . . 2022. A total of 1766 consecutive days.

If that makes you feel bad, just think of it like this: The beauty consultant would work her full 37 year career to earn a million dollars. Her boss would be a million dollars richer after five and a half days. Does that make you feel any better?

If you are the cynical type, no, I did not cherry pick this one example. Estée Lauder was the first and only company I tested.

Network Marketing is a pyramid. The United States economy is pyramid. Canada's economy is a pyramid. The global economy is a pyramid. Estée Lauder is a pyramid. I got news for ya, pretty much every organization is a pyramid, and the only people griping about it are those at the bottom.

What if there was a pyramid where you didn't have to be at the bottom? Let's consider your options with a look at the Network Marketing pyramid . . .

9. More about Network Marketing and Pyramids

Some Network Marketers try to downplay the pyramid aspect of the business compensation plan. I think this is a mistake. After all, natural, organic growth happens in the shape of a pyramid: one cell splits into two, those two split to four, four to eight, etc.; one plant produces multiple seeds; draw out your ancestry (or do it online) and you will discover that your so-called family *tree* is actually a family *pyramid*. In fact, if you really want to blow your mind, next time you look at the March Madness brackets, just turn your head sideways. How much money have you lost in *that* pyramid scheme?

If Network Marketing is a pyramid and, as we discovered earlier, most other companies are pyramids, then what is the difference? The differences are in how you succeed (advance in rank and pay) in each system.

Before investigating the criteria for promotion and pay in the two systems, let's take a quick look at the language used in Network Marketing and compare it to the language of most industries.

For this fun exercise ("fun exercise" . . . you don't often hear those two words together), I will present common terms with their definitions and then use a simple sentence to expand on their meanings. I know this may seem stupid, but bear with me – you will find it enlightening.

In Network Marketing, your position is relative to your *upline* and your *downline*. By definition, *upline* means, "those who came before you in your genealogy." Correspondingly, *downline* means "those who came after you."

Consider the following sentence:

Your sponsor is your upline; you are downline of your sponsor.

Using the above definitions, this sentence would read,

"Your sponsor came before you; you came after your sponsor."

The terms upline and downline indicate a chronological order only. One cannot draw any conclusions regarding skill level, intelligence, rank, income level, merit, or hierarchy, etc. How does this compare to the average company?

The terms that communicate one's position in a conventional company are *superiors* ("higher in station, rank, degree, importance; above in excellence, merit, intelligence; higher quality, above or better than others"), and *subordinates* ("belonging to a lower order or rank; of less importance; under the authority of a superior; subservient; inferior; dependent").

Similar to the sentence used above, consider the following:

Your boss is your superior; you are subordinate to your boss.

Using the definitions of the two words, this sentence would read:

"Your boss is more important than you due to his higher rank, better merit, and greater intelligence; you are less important, subservient, inferior to, and dependent on your boss."

Clearly, your boss is smarter and more important than you are. What a swell guy – no wonder you depend on him so much. You should send him flowers just for putting up with you all these years.

To expand on this idea, in Network Marketing, who makes more money, the upline person or the downline person? To use my wife as an example, currently she out-ranks her three immediate upline people, and earns more per month than one of them. Additionally, at the rate things are going, my wife's income may soon exceed the other two (and/or someone from my wife's downline could surpass her). This phenomenon of a downline person having a higher rank and/or earning more than people in her upline is not uncommon in Network Marketing.

How does this compare to you and/or your wife at your workplaces? Do either of you have a more prestigious title than your boss? Do either of you make more money than your supervisor, or his manager, or his manager's boss? Is there much chance of this changing any time soon?

Now that you know what people at work think of you and where you fit in the hierarchy, let's use a story about newlyweds, Betty and Barney, to explore how to earn more money in both systems.

After returning from their honeymoon, Barney gets an entry level job at the quarry and Betty signs up with a Network Marketing company that sells health products.

Barney works on a crew of 10. There are six crews altogether and each crew has a supervisor. Above the supervisors are two managers that report to the president. This means, there are 60 workers, six supervisors, two managers, and one president – a pyramid.

For Barney to earn a promotion or significant raise, one of the supervisors would have to leave the company. After two years, one finally does. Barney competes with dozens of coworkers and many outside applicants for the vacant position. He is unsuccessful. Until another supervisor leaves, Barney has no opportunity for promotion within his company so while he waits, he watches for opportunities in other companies.

Pay and promotion in this type of pyramid structure is determined by how close you are to the top (closer to top equals higher rank and higher pay); your career, therefore, is essentially in the hands of those above you. Compare this with Barney's wife.

When Betty signs up with the Network Marketing company, her upline has twelve people. Some that came before her make lots of money, others make very little. Betty is unaware of this. She just wants to use the health products, and since she signed up with the company, she gets to buy them at wholesale. Betty never plans to sell the products.

After using the products for a few weeks, however, Betty tells a few of her friends about how her health has drastically improved. Those friends sign up, buy products, get good results, and tell a few more friends. Before she knows it, Betty gets a small cheque from her company.

Intrigued, Betty asks her sponsor why she got the cheque. Her sponsor replies, "In Network Marketing, the number of people above you doesn't matter, you get paid based on the total amount of product purchased by the people in your downline. The more people you have *below* you, the larger your cheque will be."

These examples provide the basic explanation as to why Network Marketing appeals to so many people. In traditional businesses, a person has no control over how many people are above him (and therefore very little control over his rank or pay), the actions of those above him (if they choose to stay or leave the company), or the actions of the company (if they hire from the outside).

Conversely, in Network Marketing, a person has considerable control over how many people are below her, and therefore, significant control over her rank and pay. The actions of her upline (whether they stay with the company or not), makes very little difference. Network Marketers can also be assured no one will come in from the outside and hinder their opportunity for advancement. In fact, the opposite is true. Anyone who comes in from the outside joins their downline and *provides* the advancement.

What are the implications of the different structures?

In a normal corporate structure, coworkers are competing for limited positions. Meanwhile, supervisors could easily fear being passed over by subordinates or threatened by the possibility of being usurped by outside hires. This type of structure is conducive for back-biting, sabotage, withholding of information, and other negative actions that could help people gain an advantage over their competitors – and pretty much everyone is a competitor.

On the contrary, Network Marketing is built upon cooperation, not competition. Your wife's upline wants nothing more than for your wife to succeed, because when your wife succeeds, her upline succeeds. The same is true for your wife and her downline – the more she helps the people below her, the more levels are added, and the more money she makes. Because the compensation plan rewards everyone for the same thing (volume of downline sales), the need for competition is virtually eliminated. Instead, cooperation becomes in everyone's best interest. As you can imagine, this makes for a much more pleasant work environment.

Now, you may be wondering, *if Network Marketing is so great, why are there stories of people who lost all their friends after they joined an MLM company?* Good question, let's look at that . . .

10. Will we Lose all our Friends?

One of the top concerns men have about their wives (or themselves) becoming involved with a Network Marketing company is the fear they will lose all their friends. Let me just settle that right now.

No, you will not lose your all your friends.

No, no, no, no, no.

Well, maybe.

Does this sound familiar: Friends stop answering your calls, you are rarely invited out as a couple any more, your family, who always used to come over for Sunday dinner, now always seems to be busy, what happened?

Your wife became a zealot, that's what happened.

I have done some intense research and – get this – it turns out that most people do not enjoy being continually harassed. They don't appreciate being bombarded with Network Marketing opportunities, essential oils, your kid's eighth fundraiser this month, or anything else for that matter.

If they are avoiding your wife, she should probably take the hint. They are obviously sick of hearing about how their J.O.B. (old Network Marketing insult meaning, "just over broke") will keep them poor forever and how they need to start a Network Marketing business. They are tired of hearing how marvellous the oils are, how they need oils, and how they are complete idiots if they don't start using oils, and . . . you get the picture.

If your wife has yammered nonstop about the oils or the business opportunity to the point that you are losing relationships, you have two options: First, thank your wife for repulsing her own family so much that they no longer call or stop over – something you have been trying to accomplish since you got married. Or, if ditching your in-laws is not worth losing all your other family and friends, politely invite her to *shut up about the oils around these people!*

When you gently tell your wife to zip her lip, she may argue that if she does not share the oils, her business will die. It doesn't have to. There are ways to share the oils and the business that do not repel people. She can learn skills that get people to ask her about her products and request a presentation. Many of these techniques are rejection-proof so they don't make your wife feel awkward and, best of all, they won't cost you your friends.

She may not believe you when you suggest there might be a better way (after all, what do you know? You've never been in MLM), so ask her to think about this: Pretty much everyone wants three things:

    1) More money,

    2) More time, and,

    3) Better health.

Your wife is offering people an opportunity to get all three things they want, yet they are avoiding her like the plague. Is there a chance she might be doing something wrong?

For the sake of your friends and family – and to support your wife's success – help her learn skills so the people who choose to, can benefit from what she has to offer, and the rest won't run when they see her coming.

We have discovered that there are ways to be successful at Network Marketing without losing all your friends, but some guys are uneasy about another aspect of friendships. These fellas don't think you should make money off your friends. This, too, is worth investigating . . .

11. Is it Wrong to Make Money off your Friends?

Some guys who say they object to Network Marketing because they think it is wrong to profit off of their friends really mean it. Others mean that they do not want to push away their friends. If you are afraid you will lose all your friends because your wife is hounding them too much, go back and read the last chapter. In this chapter, I address those who don't feel comfortable making money from their friends' purchases.

It is a well-known marketing fact that the absolute best way to get someone to buy a product is a recommendation from someone the potential buyer knows, likes, and trusts. Traditional advertising relies heavily on the last two: companies pay people you like and trust to endorse their products or services.

This tactic of using celebrity endorsers that you like and trust is the reason why companies paid extremely large sums of money for people like Lance Armstrong and Bill Cosby to peddle their goods. It is also the reason why you don't see these two men in ads much anymore – it can be somewhat unsettling when someone you don't like or trust keeps offering your kid a Pudding Pop.

Network Marketing also relies on endorsements from people you like and trust, but it also adds the personal element of getting recommendations from someone you actually know. In its purest form, Network Marketing is friends telling friends about products they use and love, and then those friends begin using and sharing the products as well.

The obvious difference in the two strategies is that in traditional advertising, the person pitching the product does not know the prospect, whereas in Network Marketing, the person recommending the product usually knows the customer (or knows someone close to the customer).

The similarity between the two strategies is that companies are paying *someone* for sharing.

For example, according to Forbes, Lebron James will make nearly double for endorsing products this year than he will for shooting hoops ($55 million to $31 million). I know he wears Nikes, but I question how many Cokes he drinks, how often he drives a Kia, and how many Dunkin Donuts he has consumed (all current or recent endorsement deals). Regardless, he seems to believe all of these things would be good for you and me to do more often.

In 2017, Nike paid eight NBA players a total of $100 million to sport the swoosh.

Do you think that may be part of the reason you just paid $150 for your kid's $20 high tops?

Your wife (probably) doesn't have a lion/dragon tattoo on her chest, she (probably) isn't six foot eight, and she (hopefully) has never taken her talents to South Beach; but what do your wife and Lebron have in common?

Your wife and Lebron are both side hustling: earning some extra cash by recommending products to *your* friends. Whether they buy the Coke and donuts Lebron is pushing, or they buy your wife's Lavender and Peppermint oil, someone is making money off your friends.

When determining what is acceptable, is there a chance we have been influenced by ad-agencies and/or celebrities?

Nike can heap truckloads of money onto Lebron's mountainous pile of cash and we don't make a peep, yet Young Living pays your wife's friend – the single mom in the one bedroom apartment – $300 a month for selling oils and suddenly, *it's just not right for her to make money off her friends?* Does this seem rational to you?

I recently heard an amusing story that makes me think the apparent disdain for profiting off friends may sometimes just be an excuse:

Someone I know was suffering from back issues. Fortunately, she has a friend who is a massage therapist, so she went in for a massage. During the massage, they got talking and the masseuse said, "I really like essential oils and I use them all the time, but I don't want to do Network Marketing – you shouldn't make money off your friends." When the massage concluded, the friend paid the masseuse (plus tip) and left. Hmmm.

Maybe you now realize that your concern was not with making money off your friends, but you now discover that deep down you have integrity (who knew?) and don't want your wife to swindle or take advantage of your friends.

If so, I completely agree.

If your wife does not truly believe in the products/opportunity that she is selling, she should not be trying to sell them to others. To do so would be the same as a pacifist selling guns, an environmentalist using plastic water bottles . . . or a professional athlete telling us to eat donuts – it just wouldn't be right.

Speaking of money, it is time to investigate the different ways a person can earn money, and reveal why some ways are better than others. If you have ever had concerns about money for retirement, I think you are going to like this . . .

12. What is Passive Income and why does it Matter?

How you earn your money determines what, if any, limits there are on the amount you can make. There are two ways to earn income: actively and passively.

Active income is money you earn by doing something. You trade your time for money. Regardless of the amount you earn, the way you can tell if income is active income is to ask, *if I didn't do anything* (this week, this year, or ever), *would I still get paid?* If you would stop being paid, you are earning active income.

Active income earners are usually paid by the hour, by the job, or they earn a set yearly salary. Some examples of jobs where one earns active income are:

-   Cashier
-   Construction worker
-   Professional basketball player
-   Medical doctor
-   Prison Warden
-   Rodeo clown

As you can see, the amount you can earn through active income may be small or large, but it is limited by the number of hours you are willing and able to work.

Passive Income, on the other hand, is money that comes in while you do nothing. Some examples of passive income are:

-   Interest on your bank account and other financial investments (GICs, Treasury Bills, Bonds, etc.)
-   Dividends from your stock portfolio
-   Pensions
-   Cashflow from your rental properties (after all expenses are paid)

- Royalties from that hit rock song you wrote in the '90s (or books, patent licenses, etc.)
- Lottery winnings paid out as an annuity (equal installments every month or year)

Money from these sources comes to you regardless of if you get out of bed or not, so there is no limit on the amount of passive income you can earn.

Ultimate test of passive income: Death.

If death itself does not stop your cashflow, you know you've got passive income. Check out what these dead guys earned this past year:

- Einstein (died 1955), earned $10 million;

- John Lennon (died 1980): $12 million;

- Dr. Seuss (died 1991): $16 million;

- Bob Marley (died 1981) rolled in $23 million;

- Elvis (died 1977) raked in a cool $35 mil;

- Arnold Palmer (died 2016): $40 million; and

- Michael Jackson (died 2009) earned over $75 million dollars from beyond the grave.

Most people go to work every day because their passive income is less than their current expenses; therefore, they need active income to make up the difference. The month your passive income meets (or exceeds) your monthly expenses, you are free to retire.

To achieve this freedom [when you say *freedom*, do you sigh it out like, "Ahhh, *freedom*," or, do you shout it rebelliously with a Scottish accent like William Wallace in Braveheart, "*FREEDOM!*"?], you have three choices:

1. Receive a windfall (a large inheritance or win the lottery).
2. Build up a large portfolio of financial investments and cash so you can live off the dividends and interest.
3. Build a business that provides you with the required amount of monthly passive income.

If you have a childless rich uncle or an inside track on how to win the Powerball, I wish you all the best (and I wonder why you read this far). If, however, you will need to use either strategy #2 or strategy #3, you will want to read on . . .

13. The Rule of 200

You are about to learn the reason why you should give your wife's Network Marketing side hustle serious consideration. Read carefully, it could change your life (and please do not take any of this as financial advice, consult a financial advisor, blah, blah, blah*).

[*I am not a financial advisor. Statements of earning potential made in this book are for informational purposes only and not to be construed as normal or guaranteed. Actual results will vary. Success in Network Marketing and amount of interest earned on investments depends on many factors.]

First, calculate how much money you need each month to live a lifestyle that is acceptable to you and your family. Regardless of if you earn your money through active or passive income, this number represents your monthly expenses and, therefore, your minimum monthly income requirement.

Got it?

Good.

To determine your best retirement strategy, let's use three examples. Assume you calculated your monthly income requirements as one of the following amounts:

1) $1,000/month,

2) $5,000/month, or

3) $10,000/month.

To determine how much investments/cash you must accumulate so you can live off the interest (6%), take your estimated monthly expenses and multiply that number by 200.

For example, to earn $1,000 income/month, you need to have about $200,000 ($1000 x 200) saved up.

For $5,000/month, you need $1 million in savings.

For, $10,000/month, you must have $2 million dollars in savings before you could retire.

These numbers are not exact, but they give you a good idea of what you must accumulate if you plan to retire and live off the interest.

[Side note: I only used $1,000/month as an example. If you chose this as your retirement amount, the money you save by eating cat food for all your meals will quickly be consumed on health care trying to recover from eating cat food every meal. In most circumstances, 5,000 to $10,000/month would provide most people with the retirement they dream about and deserve.]

Using the Rule of 200, you now have your first retirement savings option:

Plan A: Put money into a retirement savings plan each month. Once you reach one to two million dollars, you are free to invite your boss to cram it.

If saving one or two mill does not seem feasible to you, your second option is to build a side business that provides you with enough passive income to cover your expenses. Your two most likely options for this path are real estate or Network Marketing. If you have the time, financial resources, and knowledge, real estate investment can be a profitable venture. I say, "Go for it!"

Lack of these resources (especially money), however, is the reason most people consider Network Marketing to be their best option for creating passive income.

In Network Marketing, it is possible to create a passive income of five or ten thousand dollars a month working part time for three to five years (see Chapter 28). Network Marketing, therefore, provides you with a possible second retirement option:

Plan B: Your wife works part time for three to five years to create sufficient passive income for life.

While there are no guarantees with either option, review your wife's two choices:

1) Let's say she earns $25/hour at her job. Let's also assume that she can work as much overtime as she likes. For overtime, she earns time and a half: $37.50/hour ($28.13 after 25% tax). If, for the next 25 years she works 15 hours of overtime *every single week* (including during the summer and over Christmas), and saved every single cent (at 6% interest), she will accumulate about $1.2 million in savings. This is enough to generate a passive income of about $6000/month for your golden years.

1) Her other choice is to devote her time to building her Network Marketing business. According to the Young Living Income Disclosure Statement (shown on page 122), those earning an average of $6000/month took about 5 years.

Which plan is better for you?

While you think about that, if you really want to pile on the cash, there is a Plan C that might be of interest:

Plan C: Combine Plan A and Plan B.

In this plan, your wife would work part time in Network Marketing. Rather than spending the extra income, the two of you transfer her earnings into an investment plan or rental houses. In five or ten years, you may just have both the five to 10 thousand dollars in passive income from her Network Marketing business *and* a million dollars in investments. Freedom times two.

Sound too good to be true? After all, most people fail at Network Marketing, right? I think this is my favourite objection because when people stop and think for a minute, they quickly realize how ridiculous it is. It's like a woman blaming the mirror if she doesn't like what she sees in the reflection. Wanna see what I mean? Read on . . .

14. Don't most People Fail at Network Marketing?

Maybe you've read blogs by people who are adamant that most people fail in Network Marketing. Apparently confirming these negative sentiments, the income disclosure statements for most Network Marketing companies seem to reveal that the majority of members earn squat. And, who could forget your dear Uncle Shamus and his disastrous venture into MLM? As he loudly reminds you every Thanksgiving after a few too many adult beverages, "I stell 'ave fide 'undred dollurs worth ah *crep* en meh basemen' frum 1986!" It's a reasonable question: don't most people fail at Network Marketing? Let me tell you a story . . .

Many (many, many) years ago, when I was younger, eagerer, impressionabler, and stupider, I was watching the Winter Olympics on TV. For some bizarre reason (that I am sure made sense to me at the time), I thought cross-country skiing looked like a lot of fun. Living in a place that has no shortage of snow and flat prairie land, I thought it would be the perfect way for me to get out, have some fun, and to get some exercise.

I went out to my local sporting goods store and bought the boots, poles, and skis for about $300 (this was back before we needed a helmet just to cross the street). I also received some pointers from Jeff, the enthusiastic salesman who had cross-county skied for over two decades and was a ski coach on weekends. I was ready to go.

The next day, I could not believe my luck when I awoke to find it had snowed four inches overnight (not that miraculous since where I live it snows four inches a night about 300 days a year – at least it feels like it does). It was the perfect day for my cross-country skiing debut.

I loaded my equipment into the trunk of my car and drove to the golf course that, from about September to May, doubles as a cross-country ski area. Encouraged by the skiing enthusiasts who were already elegantly swooshing their way out the par 4 hole 1, I headed out to the tee box and strapped on my gear.

It did not go well. Turns out, Olympic athletes can make difficult things look exceptionally easy. Down I went! Getting up out of fresh snow with skis on is not fun. Down again! Why wasn't I wearing a helmet? It was funny at first (not to me, but those watching seemed amused), and I tried to laugh it off, but it quickly degraded into several (hundred) expletives. Even by golf course standards, it was incredibly frustrating.

What made my incompetence even more difficult to accept, was that I was actually quite athletic (back off, this was a long time ago). I had played high level hockey, football, and baseball. I was a decent golfer, and in a pick-up basketball or volleyball game, I would be picked near the top. At cross-country skiing, however, I sucked. Suuucked.

After this debacle, what do you think I did?

I quit.

Dejected, I removed my skis and sulked back to my car. When I arrived home, I threw, (yes, threw) the poles, the boots, and the skis into the corner of the garage. That is where my used-once $300 cross-country ski equipment sat for over a decade. I finally got rid of all of it when a heavily bearded dude with a pony tail from a charity I didn't like came by asking for "gently used items."

"Let this poor tree-hugger suffer like I did," I thought as I passed the equipment over to the appreciative yet naïve hippie at my door. My foray into cross-country skiing was officially over.

Let's review.

For 10 years, $300 worth of gear that I used only once was collecting dust in my garage; did the sporting goods store rip me off?

Second, I tried skiing and then I gave up; did I fail at cross-country skiing?

The answer to both questions is, of course, *no*. The equipment was perfectly adequate. I am sure any of the Olympians I had watched could have skied just fine with them (with their long graceful strides and rock-hard abs – I hate them so much). The problem was that I did not want to devote the time it would have taken to become proficient. I quit. I did not fail at cross-country skiing, I quit. I quit, and that is okay.

Fail or Quit?

Fail: "[In business] to become unable to meet or pay debts or business obligations; become insolvent or bankrupt"

Quit: "To stop, cease, give up, or resign"

We all only have so much time, energy, and money in life, so we have to choose carefully the things we are willing to devote our limited resources to. While I was making a fool of myself trying to cross-country ski on a golf course (hmm, when I read that over, I probably should have anticipated trouble), I realized I did not want to pay the price necessary to learn to be successful. That's it.

I can't blame the equipment. I can't blame Jeff (although he really should have sold me a helmet – is it too late to sue?). I can't blame the golf course or the snow (other people were skiing that day). I can only blame myself.

Think about it, failure requires an outside constraint – usually a time deadline – that *forces* a person to stop before achieving success. Quitting, on the other hand, is a choice.

To win a football game, for example, a team has to score more points than their opponent *before* time runs out, or they fail to win. A student must learn the information *before* the exam, or he fails the test. A businessman must have enough money available *before* the bills are due, or he fails in business.

Without a time constraint, it is difficult to even imagine failure – how could you lose a football game if you were the one to decide when it was over?

Quitting, on the other hand is a choice a person makes. If you are in the position where you can choose to stop or choose to continue (even if continuing would be difficult), and you choose to stop, you have not failed, you have quit. I no longer ski because I chose to quit.

Most of the people with sad stories about unopened products and being out $200 (or $500 like Unkie Shamus) were not forced to stop, so they did not fail. They made a choice to do something different with their time. They do not need to feel guilty about quitting; they just didn't want to devote the time and effort it would take to succeed. Like skiing, Network Marketing is not for everyone.

Caveat: I have heard people say that the only way you can be unsuccessful in Network Marketing is to quit. In other words, never quit, and you will (eventually) succeed. Nah, I don't buy it.

Most of the people who hear this "never quit" mantra seem to assume that it means, never stop going to meetings, never stop having strategy meetings with your sponsor, never stop "liking" your upline's Facebook posts, and most of all, never stop hoping. While these things are all good, her not quitting these things probably won't get you that new Porsche.

These activities will keep your wife in her Network Marketing community, but they won't build her business. I could have not quit updating my skis, not quit watching motivational videos on skiing, not quit reading salesman Jeff's blog (had such a thing existed in the 90s), and not quit hoping I would be an Olympic skier, but I still would have sucked.

To succeed, I would have had to not quit learning skills and not quit perfecting them by getting out there and doing the work. This same dedication is what it will take for people who want to build a Network Marketing business. Some people act like this is a lottery – just pay your $150 a month and "hope this works!" No, you learn and *you* work.

What does it take to succeed in Network Marketing? Same as what it takes to become a good skier:

  1) Develop the right mindset,

  2) Have the proper equipment/products,

  3) Learn and master skills by doing them . . . over and over and over again.

If your wife spends all her time focussing on only one of these three areas (often the second one, because she probably loves the products), she may not quit, but she likely won't succeed.

While sticking around does not guarantee victory, however, quitting will absolutely eliminate any chance for success. If you want to send your former coworkers a picture of you on the beach showing off your one-size-too-small Speedos, your wife cannot be one who quits. Why will she quit? I'm glad you asked . . .

15. What will make my Wife Quit?

Research has shown that your wife will most likely quit building her Network Marketing business for one of two reasons:

1) She does not know what to do.

Not knowing what to do has caused many people to quit. There are two common times for this to happen:

Quitting because she does not know what to do will most often happen between six months and a year. Your wife signs up, loves the products, and tells a few friends. The friends also sign up. Your wife hits Star, gets a cheque from the company, and declares herself a "business builder." Ahh, the honeymoon stage.

A few months go by. Your Star still loves the products, but of the four people who signed up under her, three no longer buy anything. Your wife does not know what to do and so she quits (personally, I would not say she quit – she never actually started).

The second common time for quitting shares a very similar scenario, except the honeymoon stage is longer.

In this scenario, your wife signs up the same four people, then three more, then eight more, then seven more . . . until after a year and a half, she now has 79 people in her downline, she has reached Executive, and her monthly cheque may almost reach four digits.

Unfortunately, she has exhausted her friends, family, and coworkers. All the things she had been doing to gain success no longer work and she has run out of people to talk to. Her business does not die off immediately, but each month her downline shrinks a little bit, her sales volume dwindles, and eventually, her cheque gets lower than the amount of her monthly product order. Dejected, she quits. She cancels her autoship, and calls it another MLM failure.

The reality of both of these situations is that Network Marketing requires skills that must continually be developed. Some say that Network Marketing is really a personal development program disguised as a business opportunity.

Your wife bought you this book,

return the favour –

buy her Eric Worre's book, *Go Pro*.

The name says it all.

The difference between the above scenarios is that in the example your wife came in with more previous skills and/or bigger network and/or was willing to learn a few additional techniques to help her. Regardless, *the point where your wife will quit is shortly after the time she stops learning and practicing new skills.* This might happen right from the get-go, or it could happen after three years.

Your wife has to remember that she is an entrepreneur now, not an employee. It is her business – success is her responsibility. Many women have the business building "strategy" of hoping they will win the jackpot and get a few superstars in their downline. Entrepreneurs, on the other hand, decide what they want and then do what it takes to *become* the superstar [btw, my wife thought this last sentence was the best line in the book].

The fact remains, when a person stops growing their skill set, they won't know what to do and they stop building their organization. If your wife sits on a plateau too long, she will quit.

2) The second most likely reason your wife will quit (brace yourself for this one)? She will quit because of you.

OK, not just you, she will quit because of people in her life who discourage her from pursuing her oil business. It could be friends who doubt her, coworkers who question her, or family members who mock to her.

As mentioned previously, Network Marketing (and maybe even entrepreneurship in general) is likely very new to your wife. Not only is she learning and growing, she is doing it in public for all to witness her short-comings and mistakes. As she is extremely vulnerable during this process, it is little wonder that she found your (I am sure hilarious) jokes about being a witch doctor less than amusing.

Compounding this problem is that, *like any new business*, the beginning stage is when your wife will be doing the most work for the least reward. **In the early stages of Network Marketing, your wife will put in more time and work harder than she is being paid for – expect it.**

Soon, her compensation will be about right. Then, if she persists, her income will shift more to passive income and she can earn much more than the amount of effort she puts in. Without both you and her having a long-term perspective early on, however, she will be vulnerable to criticism and discouragement that will make quitting easy.

Unfortunately, many women leave Network Marketing feeling like a failure when all it would have taken to succeed beyond their dreams was having support as they learned the skills. While I do not believe a person requires the encouragement of others to succeed, the support and reassurance from a loved one speeds up the process of success and makes the journey much more enjoyable – and profitable – *for everyone*.

I was going to conclude this chapter by suggesting that your wife can succeed with you, or in spite of you, but that would be misleading. It would be extremely rare for a woman to succeed in spite of her husband – your wife will only take your crap for so long before she quits. You will be proven right ("see, it didn't work"), but it will be a hollow victory.

Part 2: Essential Oils

Now that you understand Network Marketing, you may see the opportunity for your wife to bring in some extra coin on the side. Perhaps, though, you think essential oils are bogus. In this section, I investigate essential oils, answer the snake oil question once and for all, and explore the usefulness and potential drawbacks of essential oils.

Let's start at the beginning . . .

16. What are Essential Oils?

The first question a man usually has when his wife brings home essential oils is, *How much did you blow on these?*

The second question is, *What the heck are essential oils?* (if married longer than three years, he has likely learned not to ask the first one out loud). This chapter answers the second question (on page 132 you will find out how to get the answer to the first).

There are dozens of types of oils, including:

Vegetable Oil: Taken from vegetables and used in cooking; may be utilized to promote heart disease.

Crude Oil: Taken from the ground and used to make fuel and lubricant for our toys in the garage; oil that uses vulgar language.

Midnight Oil: Taken from Australia and used to produce the 1987 hit song, "Beds are Burning."

Essential Oil: Taken from plants and contain the essence of the plant from which it was extracted; possible source of contention in your home.

People have used essential oils medicinally, cosmetically, and erotically for thousands of years. Today, the two main uses of essential oils are in the manufacturing of perfumes and flavors.

Frankincense and Myrrh are two of the most universally recognized essential oils for health and wellness; some believe that when given with gold, they are the perfect gifts

Essential oils are extracted from plants through various methods including distillation, expression, and solvent extraction. The extraction process is extremely important in preserving the quality and purity of the oil. As with most things, maintaining high quality costs money, so beware of cheap essential oils – all essential oils are not created equal (more on this later).

One obstacle guys often encounter when they go to talk about, let alone use, essential oils, are the girlish sounding names. Face it, *Citronella* and *Citrus Fresh* just don't pack the manly punch of an *Advil* or a *Gravol*.

We all know that when a husband is out working on his Harley and burns his forearm on the muffler, the last thing he wants is for his neighbors to hear his wife telling him to "sprinkle on a few drops of lavender."

To overcome this, I sometimes use the chemical names of the oils. This way, when I have a sore shoulder (probably from wrestling a bear), rather than "gently dabbing on some Wintergreen" like a little baby, I rip off my shirt and "work in some methyl salicylate!"

Knowing what essential oils are, now you want to know if they work, right? Because, really, man to man you ask, *isn't this stuff just snake oil?*

I think the answer will surprise you . . .

17. Are Essential Oils just "Snake Oil"?

This is just snake oil.

When a woman first introduces essential oils to her husband/boyfriend, she can pretty much expect to hear these words – so you were not alone when you said it to your wife/girlfriend. In fact, the only women who don't hear this comment from their husband/boyfriend are women who don't have a husband/boyfriend. In these cases, it is customary for a dad or son to step up and fill the void.

When faced with this snake oil accusation, women draw upon all the essential oil knowledge they accumulated during the 90 minute class they attended the previous evening and confidently shoot back with, "They are not!" Stomp, stomp, slam! Looks like yet another apology is in order.

While waiting for her to come out of the bathroom and say sorry, the best thing to do is just go watch baseball highlights (well, I'm not sure it's the *best* thing, but no husband has tried anything different).

So, who is right, the men (snake oil) or the women (not snake oil)? Drum roll . . .

Men. Duh.

Essential oils are snake oil (be cool – act like you've been here before).

Before I explain, if your wife has been reading this book over your shoulder, she is likely heading out the door right now with my address in one hand and a rope in the other. Do me a solid and stop her (I told her this book was not for her – and they say *men* don't listen!).

Why do I say essential oils are snake oils?

I have a quick (and true) story for you (bear with me, I used to be a high school History teacher) . . .

. . . The year was 1849, and, in America, the Gold Rush was on. To get people and supplies out West more quickly, work began on the Transcontinental Railroad. Apparently lured by the promise of long days, back-breaking toil, and low pay, tens of thousands of Chinese immigrants arrived to lay the track.

Among the items the Chinese workers brought with them to America was an ancient concoction made from the oil of the Chinese Water Snake. After a gruelling day of harsh physical labour, the workers would rub the oil on their aching muscles and joints and it would relieve their pain. Before long, the Chinese workers shared the healing oil with their American counterparts and the reputation for snake oil as a powerful pain reliever spread, along with the railroad, across the country.

There you have it, the history of how snake oil became popular across North America.

I know what you are thinking: *What are you talking about, Hall? Snake oil isn't a legendary pain reliever; it's a rip off ointment peddled by travelling cons!*

As Paul Harvey used to say, here is . . . *the rest of the story* . . .

. . . By the latter part of the 19th century, the railroad was complete and most of the Chinese immigrants had returned home. Enter Clark "the Rattlesnake King" Stanley. Not letting the fact that there were no Chinese Water Snakes in the American West stand in the way of him making a buck, Stanley figured out a way to exploit the positive reputation of the Chinese Snake Oil. Stanley created and sold his version of the traditional ointment: *Stanley's*

Snake Oil. Rather than being formulated from the oil of Chinese Water Snakes, however, Stanley brewed his tonic from Rattlesnake oil.

In 1906, the U.S Pure Food and Drug Act prohibited the interstate marketing of "adulterated" drugs, in which the "standard of strength, quality, or purity" of the active ingredient was not stated clearly on the label.

Since they are not considered drugs, however, this does not apply to essential oils.

Because the oil extracted from rattlesnakes contained less than one third the amount of the crucial healing ingredient found in Chinese Water Snakes (*eicosapentaenoic acid* for you science nerds), Stanley's concoction was far less effective than the original version. Worse yet, by the time authorities prosecuted *the Rattlesnake King* in 1917, Stanley had gone one step further, replacing the rattlesnake oil with turpentine. Thanks to this charlatan (and a few copycats), the illustrious reputation of the Chinese Snake Oil was forever tarnished.

Since Stanley's fraudulent behavior over a century ago, any unfamiliar product that salesmen claim has health-promoting qualities has been referred to as *snake oil*.

You can now see why essential oils are snake oils. In spite of being in use for thousands of years, essential oils are relatively unfamiliar to Western society. Additionally, like snake oils of the past, some essential oils being sold are high quality, pure oils that are legit health products, while others are inferior and/or diluted, and therefore, much less effective. Worse still, reminiscent of the final version of Stanley's Snake Oil, some products being marketed as 100% pure essential oils are outright fraudulent.

This brief history lesson explains why essential oils are snake oils. Now the question becomes, how do you know if an essential oil is like the Chinese Snake Oil (contains quality ingredients that work), or if it is like Stanley's Snake Oil (uses little or no effective ingredients)? I will explore this question in the next chapter.

18. How Can You Tell the Quality of an Essential Oil?

Without a lab set-up for testing, determining the quality of an essential oil can be tricky. So what's a fella to do? Let's take this from essential oils (something new and freaky) to automotive (something we actually understand).

> *"There are . . . no standards for therapeutic-grade essential oils set by any government agency in North America. Hence, labeling fraud is rampant."*
>
> Dr. David Stewart, *The Chemistry of Essential Oils Made Simple*

Have you ever bought engine coolant/antifreeze for your vehicle? Where I am from, you have two options: concentrated (undiluted) and 50/50 coolant/water mix.

A gallon of pure coolant costs about $20 and a gallon of mixed (½ coolant and ½ water) will set you back $12.

Ponder this scenario:

You need coolant and you want the concentrated version. When you arrive at AutoZone (or Canadian Tire if you are a hoser north of the border like I am), there are only two bottles left. Unfortunately, the labels have fallen off both jugs so, except for the price tags, they look identical. One costs $20 and one costs $12. What can you conclude?

You can easily determine that the $12 jug cannot be pure coolant because, at that price, it must be diluted.

What about the $20 bottle? This could be what you are after. It could be concentrated coolant, but it could also be overpriced mixed coolant.

You then spot another bottle for $8. Looks like a great deal, maybe you should buy that one?

It is really a no-brainer. The only jug that *could be* 100% pure coolant is the $20 one. I am sure you see how this relates to essential oils.

When determining quality, your decision begins with price. If they are cheap, producers have used something to dilute the pure essential oil. What is a little scary, however, is that unlike coolant where you know what it has been mixed with (water), there is no way of knowing what cheap essential oil brands have used to adulterate their oils.

Single Oil vs Blend

A single oil is an essential oil from only one plant
(eg. Lemon, Orange, Clove, etc.)

A blend is a mixture of essential oils from several plants
(eg. Thieves contains Clove, Cinnamon Bark, Eucalyptus, and Rosemary)

I will expand on the price concern in a future chapter, but for now, here are 10 things to look for and/or do to help ensure you are using high quality oils:

1) Price. High price does not necessarily mean high quality, but low price *always* means low quality. If you are going to buy cheap, don't buy at all – more on this later.

2) Know the company. Most companies simply re-sell oils they have bought from brokers, so there is little to no assurance of quality. Since adulteration can occur at any point in the process, if the distributor is not also the grower, distiller, and packager, you must research and be comfortable with each of these links in the supply chain.

3) Bottle. If the oil comes in a bottle that is not made of glass (essential oils break down plastic), dark coloured (light degrades oil quality) and small (½ ounce (15ml) or less), it is likely poor quality.

4) Label Test #1, Latin Name. The Latin name of single essential oils should be on (or under) the label.

5) Label Test #2, Description. The essential oil label for single oils (not blends) must state, "100% pure therapeutic grade essential oil." Like price, there is a caveat to this one: If it doesn't say *100% pure therapeutic grade essential oil*, it definitely isn't; but, just because it does say it, that still may not mean it is good. In other words, if it doesn't say it, don't use it; if it does say it, it's a maybe.

6) Paper Test. Put a drop of a single oil (not a blend) on a piece of white paper and allow it to dry. *Most* pure essential oils will not leave any oily residue (they may leave resin); essential oils that have been cut with carrier oils will leave an oily stain.

7) Pour Test. This may sound odd, but essential oils are not as oily as vegetable oils. They should pour and feel more

like water than corn oil or olive oil. If you pour a couple drops on your hands and rub them together, you should not see or feel any physical sign of the oil (the smell will remain but your hands will not feel greasy).

8) Smell Test. Some companies dilute essential oils with alcohol. If you smell alcohol and/or always get a headache when you smell an oil, it is not pure essential oil. Similarly, pure essential oils do not go rancid.

9) Freeze Test. Put the bottle in the freezer, pure essential oils will not freeze, but carrier oils will.

10) Water Test. Drip essential oil into water. Pure essential oil will simply float on top of the water; if the manufacturer has added soaps or detergents, they will dissolve and create a milky residue.

The industry standard for high quality essential oils is the Young Living *Seed to Seal* Guarantee. When researching essential oil companies, measure quality control against this standard:

https://www.youngliving.com/en_CA/discover/seed-to-seal

By using these guidelines, you can now determine if the essential oil your wife is pushing on you is high quality stuff. Now the question becomes, do they work? Let's take a look . . .

19. Do Essential Oils Work?

You have established that your wife is using only high quality oils and you have flushed the rest, but who cares about quality if they don't work?

Do essential oils work?

I will give you two answers to this question.

First, there are the long-term health factors to consider:

For my whole life, I have heard of the many health benefits of broccoli. Unfortunately, I do not like the taste, smell, or texture of broccoli. Lately, however, I have not been feeling the best: low energy, bad moods, and brain fog. So, today for lunch, I ate a bunch of broccoli. I still feel terrible. I wish people would shut up about the health benefits of broccoli – it clearly doesn't work.

OK, that was not a true story (I would obviously not eat broccoli even once), but the point is that everyone knows that real health is a long term game. Eating broccoli once won't make you healthy just as eating one chocolate bar won't give you diabetes. It is what you do (or don't do) consistently that will determine your health. Even then, just because you eat broccoli every day, doesn't mean you will never get sick. If you do get sick, maybe the broccoli prevented you from getting sick five times before you actually got sick this time. It is difficult to prove the effectiveness of preventative actions.

How convenient, right? I admit, it is quite unconvincing if my response to people who say the oils don't work is for me to say, "Yeah, well, you can't *prove* they don't!"

Before you sluff off essential oils as snake oil (the bad kind), you may want to do a little research. Here are three places to start:

1) Antioxidant content (ORAC scale),

2) Oil Frequency (the vibration/wavelength) and the benefits of high frequencies, and

3) The PMS oils. PMS does not mean what you think – it stands for Phenols, Monoterpenes, and Sesquiterpenes (although some oils may help with symptoms of the other PMS – hmmm, suddenly money is no object).

Additionally, the United States National Library of Medicine maintains an online database of life science and biomedical research at pubmed.gov. If you are so inclined, you can go to PubMed and read thousands of documented studies done by health professionals on the effectiveness of various essential oils.

Free radicals in the body have been linked to increased aging, diabetes, cancer, heart disease, and other ailments. The ORAC scale measures how much a food or other substance inhibits free radicals in the body. The higher the score, the better. This table provides six examples:

Substance	ORAC Score
Carrots	210
Broccoli	890
Blueberries	2,400
Vitamin E Oil	3,309
Myrrh Essential Oil	379,800
Clove Essential Oil	1,078,700

Second, the short term benefits of essential oils. As you do a little research on the long term benefits, do your own experimenting to discover short term usefulness. As a guy ages he may encounter some new challenges: any of these sound familiar: Sore joints after work? Occasional sleeplessness? Less than stellar in the sack? Muscle soreness after your beer-league game? A little hair or memory loss? Ha! I just kept adding examples even though I know you stopped paying attention after the word sack.

Here is a personal story that illustrates that not only can the oil make a difference, how you apply it may also matter.

Cedarwood is said to aid in hair growth as well as encourage sleep. To kill two birds with one stone, at bedtime, I would rub it on the top of my forehead at my hairline. I did not notice any improvement in sleep so I started rubbing it on my temples and bottom of my feet – and it was lights out!

[Sure, now I have to shave the bottoms of my feet, but it's a small price to pay for a good night sleep (kidding!)]

So, pick something that is giving you grief. Ask your wife which oil(s) you should use (or search it online) to support your body in that area. Then, commit to using the oil as suggested for a reasonable length of time. After doing this, most people see the results and are convinced. If you do not notice an improvement, try a different oil or a different application.

Human bodies are complicated and unique. Not every oil works the same for every person all of the time. However, if you use the oils consistently, you should see the effects for yourself. To make an honest assessment, make sure you write down your symptoms and your progress, or, as I am about to show, it can be easy to miss the changes.

Women often stop by our house to pick up oils. I cannot tell you how many times a woman has stood in our doorway and told my wife some variation of the following story:

> "A couple weeks ago, my husband came home from his job complaining about sore muscles. He didn't want to use the oils because 'they're just *snake oils*.' Finally, just before bed, he gave in and let me rub Panaway [a YL essential oil blend] on his back, shoulder, and neck. The next morning, he told me that he could not remember the last time he felt so good! That evening, however, he got home from work and, once again, complained of sore muscles. Yet again, he refused to use the oils as he insisted last time was 'just a coincidence.' The next morning he woke up so sore he could hardly get out of bed. Being the stubborn jackass that he is, he still refused oil. That evening, however, he was so sore that he was 'willing to try anything.' I massaged Panaway onto him again. Five minutes later, he said he was much better, and by morning, he was almost completely back to normal! Now he continually asks me for the oils and he keeps a rollerball of Panaway with him at work."

What have you learned from this story?

Lesson #1: When you are not around, your wife calls you a jackass.

Lesson #2: Essential oils can have a quick and dramatic effect.

Lesson #3: Many people initially dismiss the effects as coincidence.

Oh, and just so I don't leave you hanging, when you go to bed tonight, if you want to sleep, try Cedarwood or RutaVaLa on the bottom of your big toes, bottom of your feet, and temples. If sleep is not your goal (wink wink), give Shutran (for you) or Ylang Ylang (for her) a whirl.

An oil popular in the bedroom is
Golden Rod

I think the Latin name for that one
is maximus erectus

Still have a little inner skeptic going? I have heard a few men ask, *If essential oils worked, wouldn't my doctor prescribe them?* I think I will just capitalize a few words and make that the title of the next chapter . . .

20. If Essential Oils Worked, wouldn't my Doctor Prescribe Them?

This is the story of your family doctor: Some years back, he decided to become a medical doctor. He enrolled in a School of *Medicine*. Most of the courses he took in *Med* School revolved around him learning how to recognize the symptoms of diseases and then treating those disease symptoms with the pre-determined *medicine*. If the *medicine* your doctor prescribes does not make you feel better, he will run more tests and prescribe another *medicine*. Your doctor practices *medicine*.

The legal term for medicine is *drug*. Here, then, is the short answer to why your doctor does not prescribe essential oils: The Food and Drug Administration (FDA) categorize essential oils primarily as *cosmetics*. The FDA also includes most essential oils on their Generally Regarded as Safe (GRAS) list for *food*. Regulators like the FDA and Health Canada do not recognize essential oils as *drugs*.

FDA definition of Drug:

A substance recognized by an official pharmacopoeia or formulary. A substance intended for use in the diagnosis, cure, mitigation, treatment, or prevention of disease. A substance (other than food) intended to affect the structure or any function of the body.

If the FDA does not recognize essential oils as medicine (drugs), it is understandable why oils are not even on the medical community's radar. Doctors practice medicine (drugs), and essential oils are not approved medicine (drugs). It is logical, therefore, that essential oils are completely absent in medical training and practice.

Standard of Care:

How similarly qualified practitioners would have managed the patient's care under the same or similar circumstances.

What if, however, your doctor is proactive, researches essential oils for himself, and discovers significant health benefits? Would he recommend them to you? It's possible. In doing so, however, he would deviate from medical regulations for *standard of care* and open himself up to a malpractice suit and/or discipline from his Medical Association.

[DISCLAIMER: No medical claims are made in this book. My doctorate is in Education, not medicine. Information provided is for educational purposes only and not to be taken as medical advice. Always do your own research and talk to a trusted healthcare professional. Now that we have that straight . . .]

Consider the following hypothetical example:

Doctor diagnoses Joe with cancer.

Scenario 1: Joe's doctor prescribes chemotherapy. Joe gets chemo. Joe dies. Joe's family sues doctor.

Because chemotherapy is the medically accepted treatment for cancer, Doc fulfilled his legal duty to Joe and the law protects Joe's doctor. Doctor goes home and has supper with his family.

Scenario 2: Based on numerous studies he has read, instead of chemo, Joe's doctor recommends Essential Oil X. Joe uses Oil X. Joe dies. Joe's family sues doctor.

Because chemotherapy, not Essential Oil X, is the standard medical treatment for cancer, a court will likely convict Joe's doctor of malpractice. The courts and/or medical associations will force him to pay an enormous fine and/or lose his medical license and/or lose his practice. Instead of having supper at home, Doc would be in court. He would almost certainly be on the news. Even if he avoids jail time, he will likely need to find a new profession.

Let's bring this home and pretend you are Joe's doctor. Assume that Essential Oil X works 99% of the time (but does not have approval) and chemo works 40% of the time. Because the medical community only endorses approved drugs, chemotherapy is still the recommended treatment. As his doctor, what would you prescribe for Joe?

Because Essential Oil X would more than double Joe's chances of survival, you may be tempted to deviate from standard of care. If you did, 99% of the time, you would have a happy Joe. Unfortunately, however, your noble career would likely come to a screeching halt after about 100 patients – when the 1 out of 100 did not survive and the family sued your stethoscope off.

Think about it, why would medical schools teach *anything* that a doctor could not utilize in his practice? They wouldn't.

The issue of standard of care is a thorny one. No doubt, regulating the actions of doctors was put in place to protect people from quacks and inhumane experiments. At the same time, however, one of the unintended consequences of regulation is that doctors are severely restricted what they can offer for treatments.

Don't assume that your doctor is giving you – or even has – *all* the information. He is probably an awesome guy who wants nothing but the best for you but, for better or for worse, regulations control your doctor.

Do your own research. Research the drugs (and side effects). Research essential oils. Research other options. Whatever you decide, make informed choices.

"Truth is not afraid of questions."

Paramahansa Yogananda

Understanding the restrictions on your doctor, questions now become about the FDA (or Health Canada) and the medical community in general. If essential oils really work, why aren't they recognized drugs?

21. Why aren't Essential Oils Recognized Drugs?

As indicated in the previous chapter, the FDA and Health Canada do not recognize essential oils as drugs, why is this?

This is a complicated question. Again, I will give you a brief answer and leave you to research this further if you have interest.

Peer review is the evaluation of work by one or more people of similar competence to the producers of the work (peers). Peer review methods are employed to maintain standards of quality, improve performance, and provide credibility.

Do a search on pubmed.gov and you will discover thousands of peer reviewed research articles that appear to demonstrate the effectiveness of essential oils. Why don't you know about this? Moreover, why aren't these essential oils approved drugs so doctors can prescribe them? Several reasons . . .

For a substance to be an approved drug, it must pass through extensive clinical trials. These trials cost tens, if not hundreds of millions of dollars.

Why, you ask, would any company go to this great expense? I will answer with an example.

In 2010, statin (cholesterol lowering) drug sales in the US were more than $19,000,000,000. This explains why pharmaceutical companies go through the time and expense to get a drug approved. *One* drug, *one* country, *one* year: 19 billion dollars.

Compare these sales to Young Living Essential Oils.

For all of their products combined, Young Living only recently surpassed 1.5 billion dollars in worldwide sales. They, like most non-pharmaceutical companies, simply cannot afford the process of obtaining FDA approval.

There is an even greater reason why Young Living cannot afford to get approval, however, and this reason may surprise you. I will illustrate with a hypothetical example.

Once again, assume that Essential Oil X did cure cancer. Now, let's say that Young Living spent a hundred million dollars to get Essential Oil X recognized as an approved drug that cured cancer.

As an approved cancer-curing drug, the FDA would then allow Young Living to market Essential Oil X as a cure for cancer and doctors would be free to prescribe it to their patients. How much would this approval be worth to Young Living?

Considering estimates for cancer treatment is currently in the neighborhood of 200 billion dollars/year, this approval should be worth billions to Young Living, maybe even trillions, right?

No, it would be worth *nothing* to Young Living. In fact, approval would probably put them out of business.

What?

Substances found in nature cannot be patented. Since essential oils are natural products, companies cannot patent them. Young Living, therefore, could not protect the product, and anyone could produce and sell the oils. Competing with companies 50 times their size would likely not end well for Young Living.

We all know that some grapes are sweet while others are bitter. This inconsistency is an unpleasant reality for you, but a big problem for the FDA.

For a drug to gain regulatory approval, each batch of the drug must be identical.

The variability of natural products makes approval for unprocessed, non-synthesized substances virtually impossible.

It takes tens of millions of dollars to get a drug approved, and companies cannot patent products found in nature. These facts explain why only synthetic drugs are submitted for FDA approval. Tying this to what we discovered last chapter, the medical community only recognizes drugs that are FDA approved, so, your doctor *has no choice but to prescribe synthetic drugs.*

Summary: Companies like Young Living that sell high quality natural products are in a catch-22 situation. Without FDA approval, they cannot market products for the cure, prevention, or treatment of disease. On the other hand, even if they were able to afford the process and prove the effectiveness of the products, approval would mean endless competition for a non-patentable product. The approval they need for legitimacy would drive them out of business.

While regulations prohibit making many positive health claims about essential oils, I am free to discuss the negatives, so I will . . .

22. Are There Side Effects to Essential Oils?

OK, if you are using an essential oil from a company that cuts/dilutes its oils with other substances – and you do not even know what those substances are – all bets are off. Of course there could be side effects. What side effects? Who knows? All I know is that when an oil is diluted, it is referred to as *adulterated* – sounds to me like something that could have nasty side effects.

What about pure, high quality, essential oils, do they have side effects?

"Everything is poison, there is poison in everything. Only the dose makes a thing not a poison"

Paracelsus, the Father of Toxicology, (1493–1541)

Some people argue that because (high quality) essential oils are all natural, there are no side effects. That seems wrong to me. If you define "side effects" as does the dictionary: *any unintended effect that is unwanted or unpleasant,* there is no question – even natural products may cause undesired effects.

If I am not mistaken, some people react poorly to natural products such as peanuts, dairy, gluten, coffee, sugar, heroin, and even water. Yes, even if a substance as healthy and vital for life as water, if used improperly or in the wrong amounts, can cause damage (think drowning, hyper-hydration, or putting your hand in front of the wand at the car wash). When using essential oils, you have to remember that the contents of these cute little bottles are very powerful and can have side effects that can bring you to your knees in a hurry if you are not careful.

This brings me to my horrific experience . . . my traumatic tale of essential oils gone wrong. Unintended, unwanted, and unpleasant consequences from essential oils. Let me tell you of agony so great that it makes women's experiences in childbirth seem like the hardships that come from eating an ice cream cone on a hot summer day (still wonder why this book is for men only?). Here is my harrowing saga – the story you have been waiting for – I call it, *Peppermint Hell*.

One morning several years ago, (when we were new to essential oils), I was lying on my bed (if you have a blanket, you can call the bathroom floor a bed), dealing with the fallout from the bad decisions I had made the previous evening.

It's probably not what you're thinking. I don't want to give too much detail – and who can say for sure what caused it – but suffice to say that when it comes to scallops, even a little expired is too expired – I don't care how much they are on sale.

Now, don't misunderstand, in spite of my pathetic appearance using the base of the toilet as a pillow, I was being brave – very brave (some might say superhumanly brave, but that's for history to decide). As my body was employing every means possible to rid itself of my poor judgement, it was apparent that my normally proficient digestive tract was in dire need of support.

Somehow, in the depths of my misery, my wife found out about my wretched condition. Perhaps she heard my moaning. Maybe one of the kids told her. There is also the outside chance she read my hysterically sarcastic tweet: "I can barely function enough to type this tweet" #nobodycares #thunderdownunder. I don't think she saw my post on Facebook: Joel is . . . "Wondering what he did to deserve such neglect from his wife." Regardless, she eagerly came to my rescue (*eagerly*, am I using that correctly?).

After consulting her Reference Guide (the book, not the psychic), my wife determined that the best way to restore my gastrointestinal health (and, more importantly, to stop the smear campaign I had launched on social media) was for me to rub peppermint essential oil on my stomach.

As I recall, after she hurled (ugh, the word *hurled* still makes me queasy) the bottle at me, with what little strength I could muster, I whispered, "Thank you for providing me with this wonderful oil. What did I ever do to deserve you? I really appreciate you and your care for me. I love you." Perhaps I was overly kind, but that is just the kind of guy I am.

She smiled sweetly at me (which, looking back, should have made me suspicious), turned, and walked out of the room (did I hear laughter?). I grasped the small bottle of peppermint oil and twisted off the lid. The sweet minty smell wafted up to my nose. It reminded me of candy canes and Christmas and . . . oh boy . . . bowels clenching . . . no time for nostalgia!

I tipped the bottle and a couple drops of oil fell onto my churning gut. Too depleted to muster the appropriate level of skepticism, I obediently massaged the oil into my skin.

Lying in the fetal position and afraid to move, I heroically waited for the peppermint oil to do its thing. As men always do in such circumstances, I distracted myself by concentrating on how awesome it is to have such a compassionate wife.

Obviously captivated by my adoration for her, I reached up and mindlessly wiped the sweat from my forehead. So began my initiation into the potential side effects of essential oils.

Immediately, a cooling sensation materialized where my hand had contacted my face. I paused as I tried to determine the cause of such an extraordinarily chilling feeling. It took me a few seconds.

Suddenly, terror gripped me as I realized what just transpired. I had rubbed my forehead with peppermint oil still on my hand. Like animals sense an approaching storm and take cover, my body tightened as it braced itself for what was to come.

The arctic menthol feeling on my forehead spread outward to my temples, crept back to my ears, and then downward, past my eyebrows . . . oh no . . . (here it comes . . .)

. . . PAIN! Pain that could not have been worse if I had injected salted ammonia and lemon juice straight into my eye sockets! How could something that felt like ice burn so horribly? I felt like there was a sadistic goalie-mask-wearing Santa Claus from some B-rated Christmas/Halloween horror movie relentlessly stabbing two well-sucked-on, pointy candy canes directly into my corneas.

The unrelenting peppermint oil did not halt until it had thrust itself deep into my skull.

Now, people who use oils often suggest applying peppermint oil on top of other oils because peppermint "acts like a hammer" to drive the other oil deeper. I think they might be on to something. You know those words you say when you hit your finger with a hammer? Yep, I said them. I said every, last, one of them.

There is no disputing it – the excruciating pain in my eyes that day was 100 times worse than labour ever could be. The only comfort was knowing the pain could not get any worse . . . and then it did.

The peppermint mixed with my tears (yes, tears. Maybe lighten up on the judgement until it happens to you), and I finally understood why my grade 8 science teacher said to never use water to put out a grease fire. The already infinite agony somehow intensified and spread.

I am not overstating it at all when I say that it was horrendous, tormenting pain – pain that was worse than any pain ever experienced by anyone, ever.

Quickly realizing I could not leave my body to escape the torture, I blindly stumbled my way to the kitchen, making promises to God the whole way. Rest assured, if I survived this, I would be committed to some orphanage building.

Somehow, valiant soldier that I am, I managed to dump some olive oil on a paper towel and press it firmly into the balls of burning that were once my eyes.

Mercifully, relief came quickly. I blinked into the olive oil soaked paper towel a few times and the pain subsided. In spite of my wife's best efforts, I had survived.

I learned three valuable lessons that day:

1) Wives do not have a sense of humour when you call them out on social media,

2) In certain circumstances, olive oil and paper towels quickly alleviate extreme pain. I, therefore, assume it could be an inexpensive alternative to epidurals during childbirth. Why has no one else thought of this? And,

3) Be careful (be very, very careful) with peppermint essential oil around the eyes. I have been assured it will not do permanent damage, but holy writhing agony, Batman!

Food allergies are rare, affecting about 2% of adults and 5% of children.

While unpleasant, most symptoms are a result of food sensitivity or intolerance, not allergies.

While my tragic tale was an extreme example, some people do experience minor issues when first using an essential oil. For example, some people have skin sensitivities and may develop a rash as the potent oil is quickly absorbed into the skin. The solution? Start slow and/or use a carrier oil (a fatty oil like coconut oil, olive oil, or Young Living's V-6 Oil) to dilute.

Although people may have reactions, I found no research indicating true allergies (immune system response) *to pure essential oils.* Allergic reactions could occur, however, if a person is allergic to filler oils (peanut oil, for example) or other additives found in some essential oil bottles. It is wise, therefore, to stick with a reputable company that sells high quality undiluted essential oils, and to start slow when introducing a new oil.

After spending this chapter dissing my wife, I should conclude it by mentioning that after the whole peppermint ordeal, my stomach was actually back to normal . . . but I think it was just a coincidence (#snakeoil).

23. Why not just buy a Cheaper Brand?

If you have read this far, you probably aren't asking this question anymore, but for those of you who have skipped ahead, I will further demonstrate why buying a cheaper brand may not be a good idea. Back to some good ol' economics . . .

Fact: For a company to remain in business, it must bring in enough money to cover its costs.

Fact: Producing and distributing products has a floor price (the absolute lowest selling price that will cover costs).

Fact: Because costs are greater, high quality products have a higher floor price than lower quality products.

Fact: Any company that sells below its floor price must soon be out of business.

Conclusion: If a product is selling for less than the floor price of a high quality product (let alone one third of that floor price) for a sustained period, it CANNOT be a high quality product.

For every one pound of frankincense distilled in the world, more than 12 pounds of "100% pure" frankincense is sold

---

You do not need to be an economist to figure this out. Which would sell for less, oil made from authentic Chinese water snakes and imported from Asia, or Stanley's Snake Oil, made from water and a splash turpentine?

The same is true of essential oils. If the price of the oil is less than what it would cost to grow, distill, package, and distribute a high quality oil, guess what? As my British Grandma used to say, "It's rubbish."

I live in Saskatchewan – a province in Western Canada.

Directions from Las Vegas to my house: Drive east to Denver. Turn Left. Drive north 1000 miles. Grey house with basketball net on driveway. You can't miss it.

If you are still tempted to take your chances and go with something that appears to be a bargain, here is a personal story about what can happen when you cheap out:

I like to fish. Here in Saskatchewan, we fish for jack (now, if you are American, you may know jack as *Northern Pike*. We use the more exotic-sounding name with Americans so lodges can charge you double when you come up here to fish – it's all marketing, baby). To catch jacks, you mainly use *spoons*.

If you are unfamiliar with fishing lingo, a spoon is a lure in which the body is similar to the portion of the large spoon that you put into your mouth when you are eating ice cream directly from the pail. It is usually painted with designs that, theoretically, make it irresistible to jack. The most common spoons are the *red-and-white*, the *five-of-diamonds*, and the *green-and-black* (love those creative names).

Attached to the body is a treble hook. A treble hook is three single J-shaped hooks soldered together back to back so it can attach to fish, fingers, or eyelids from a multitude of angles. In fact, some guides will tell you that if you catch a fish, finger, and an eyelid simultaneously, that is what we Canadians call a *Hat Trick* – but that, of course, is bull. Up here, a Hat Trick is when a player scores three goals in one hockey game – whereas the fish-finger-eyelid trifecta is just considered part of an awesome day of fishin'!

[Allow me to pause here because I know some of you Americans are still choked about the jack/Northern Pike thing. Relax. When you consider the exchange rate on the Canadian dollar, you are still getting a great deal – get up here and go fishing with me!]

Anyway, for many years, I would only buy one specific brand of spoon, the Len Thompson. Len Thompson spoons are thick, heavy, and use brass for the body and high quality stainless steel for the treble hooks (if you are wondering, no, unfortunately I have no financial interest in the company).

Each Len Thompson spoon has the name *Len Thompson* engraved into the back of it (I get the feeling Len is/was a shameless self-promoter). The thing about Len Thompson hooks, though, is that they are expensive. When I was buying hooks for myself only, I never really considered the cost and I just bought them because Len Thompsons were (are) the industry standard for spoons.

A number of years ago, however, I was forced to evaluate my spoon-buying habits. For the first time, I was taking my three young sons fishing with me, so I needed to buy a lot more hooks. It was going to cost me a bundle to stock my new family size tackle box. It was then that I made a discovery.

At my local bait shop, next to the rack of Len Thompsons, I noticed a bin of store brand spoons. They had all the classics: the *red-and-white*, the *five-of-diamonds*, and even the sometimes hard to find, *green-and-black*. Although they were a little thinner and lighter than the Len Thompsons, they looked just as shiny. Best of all, they were one third the price – score! *A hook is a hook*, I thought. So, for about the same outlay as what I used to spend on me alone, I filled up my basket with enough hooks for four of us.

Needless to say, I was quite pleased with myself.

It wasn't long into our trip, however, that I realized my mistake. Reviewing my tackle box after the first day, the paint on the store brand spoons was peeling off and, because of the poor quality steel, many of the treble hooks had bent or snapped right off. Not only were the hooks now useless, we had lost several fish when they broke. Turns out, the cheap hooks were . . . cheap. Who could have predicted that?

Adding insult to injury, to replenish my tackle box, I had to go buy some Len Thompsons from the bait shop at the lodge where we were staying – for nearly double what they cost in the city.

To make matters even worse, when the trip was over and I was cleaning up, I noticed the fine print on the packages of the store brand spoons: "Paint may contain lead." I threw away the poisonous hooks (and made a mental note to invite the in-laws over for a fish fry to eat the fish we caught on the first day). Lesson learned.

> *What does it take to get a 1/2 oz. (15 ml)*
> *of essential oil?*
>
> *Lemon Oil: 75 lemons,*
>
> *Lavender Oil: 6 pounds of lavender*
> *(approx. 27 square feet)*
>
> *Rose Oil: 40 pounds of rose petals*
> *(I've never weighed a rose petal, but that*
> *seems like a lot)*

I was reminded of this story a few months back when I was in a big-box store and I came across bottles of lavender oil for a fraction of the price of Young Living Lavender Oil. I remembered the fine print on the cheap hooks, "Paint may contain lead," and just kept walking.

If you are ok with your wife buying essential oils, but think that she should just buy them off the shelf at the store, remember the stories of the engine coolant, the worthless imitation snake oil, the lead-based, cheap, useless, crappy fish hooks, and think again. If your wife is going to buy essential oils for herself and your children (and maybe even for you), buy the good ones – save the sketchy ones for the in-laws.

24. Wouldn't Young Living Oils be Cheaper if they didn't pay Distributors so Much?

Maybe you don't question the quality of Young Living products, but you still think they would be much cheaper if the distributors were not paid such high commissions or if Young Living did not give away so many free trips and stuff.

Surprisingly, this is not the case. Way to go, you are bringing out my inner economist again . . .

Economies of Scale:

The cost advantage that arises with increased output of a product

If Young Living paid less (or gave away fewer trips), there would be significantly fewer distributors (remember incentives?) and fewer sales. Due to economies of scale, with fewer sales, the cost of producing and shipping each unit would rise. Therefore, if they paid distributors *less*, each bottle of oil would cost *more*.

Huh?

If I were an accountant, I would say that Young Living has very high *fixed* costs (land, buildings, farm machinery, distillation/packaging/labeling equipment, warehouses, etc.) and relatively low *variable* costs (employees, labels, bottles, etc.). So, once the initial investment for infrastructure is complete, producing additional oils adds relatively little to the cost.

I am not an accountant, however, so I will tell you a story instead:

Roscoe decides to go bear hunting. He plans to shoot a bear and sell the skin to his buddy, Virgil, who makes rugs. Roscoe buys all the equipment he needs for a bear hunting trip: plaid shirt, Elmer Fudd hat, gun, knife, tent, sleeping bag, camp stove, a 1998 Ford 4x4 pickup with flood lights on the roll bars, and a jar of honey for bait (it's his first time huntin' bear). The total cost is $3000.

Roscoe goes out to the woods for three days and shoots a bear. To turn a profit, he sells the pelt to Virgil for $3500.

Net result: Virgil paid $3500; Roscoe's profit, $500.

Alternatively, Roscoe could stay for three extra days of hunting and take advantage of economies of scale. Because he's already paid for his equipment, the additional costs are minimal. The three extra days cost him $1000 and he gets another bear.

Roscoe's total cost is now $4000 ($3000 + $1000).

His cost per bear is $2000 ($4000/2 bears).

Roscoe sells one of the bear skins to Virgil and the other to Virgil's half-brother, Skeeter, for $2500 each. Roscoe collects five grand and everyone is happy.

Net result: Virgil and Skeeter each paid $2500 (notice Virgil paid $1000 less in this scenario); Roscoe profited $1000 ($500 more).

Because Roscoe spent more money up front, everyone – except the bears – win (just like in the NFL). Roscoe's customers each *paid less* for their products, while Roscoe *earned more* from sales.

By paying their distributors well, and by rewarding them with trips and bonuses, Young Living sales volume goes up and prices go down.

Lesson: Do not make the mistake of thinking that high commissions lead to higher priced oils when, in fact, the opposite is true. Instead, encourage your wife to take advantage of the high commissions, sell the oils, and make some big cash. This way you can tell your (more deserving, more intelligent, and more important) boss that you will no longer be dependent on him. Then, instead of going to work on Monday, you can go do some bear hunting!

Part 3: Your Wife's Young Living Business

We have covered Network Marketing and essential oils in general and you are doing great! You have made it to the home stretch. It's time to get a little more specific.

This section will address some of your concerns about your wife's Young Living business. Let's look at the big three: Money, time, and pride . . .

25. Why is my Wife Spending so much every Month?

Ok, are you complaining about how much product she is buying to help keep her, you, and your children healthy, or are you griping because of her business expenses like giving out samples and going to Convention?

If it is the former (the first one), you have probably noticed bottles of oil all over the house. There are oils on the counter in the kitchen, on the shelf in the bathroom, next to the diffuser (the little humidifier looking thing) in the kid's bedroom, and even oils in her purse (I am sure you were just looking for keys, not cash for KFC).

These are just the oils you know about. I hate to break it to you, buddy, but she also has a stash in a drawer or box or railway container somewhere. For the record, I am with you – her hiding oils from you is *completely* different from you hiding whisky/cigarettes/chocolate bars/beer/lottery tickets/tools/new Len Thompson hooks from her. It is certainly *nothing* like that $400 you secretly spent last week at Best Buy or the 250 bucks you dropped at Bass Pro. Regardless, quite a bit of cash is going to Young Living – and you don't like it. You don't like it one bit.

There is no getting around it, health costs money. The one thing more expensive than health, though, is sickness (Yikes! I know that sounds preachy, but it's true. If you really think being sick costs less than being healthy, I envy you – you and your family members have probably never been sick). That said, health may not cost you as much as you might think.

Much of what your wife is spending on Young Living products may be offset by no longer spending money on things you used to regularly buy. Transitioning to a toxin-free home means trips to the store will no longer include buying laundry detergent, glass cleaner, veggie wash, toothpaste, hand soap, baby wipes, diaper cream, facial scrub, shampoo, conditioner, make-up, skin care products, vitamins, supplements, weight loss products, energy drinks, protein powders, granola bars, or any number of other potentially toxic or otherwise unhealthy products.

Because you are replacing these items with Young Living products, you may already be saving the $150 or so per month on your other shopping bills. These direct savings are fairly easy to see, but there are also indirect savings that are more difficult to spot.

Healthy living is like preventative maintenance on your car. Regular oil changes and transmission fluid flushes on a car that is operating perfectly can feel like a waste of time and money. The cost of those things, however, pale in comparison to the cost of replacing the motor or the transmission. In the long-run, it is much less expensive to spend the money up front, but the tough part is that you never know the damage you are avoiding – so it is easy to neglect. The same goes for the health of your family.

Once you have removed toxins from your home, you will find that you need to spend much less money on symptom relieving products such as prescriptions, Tylenol, Advil, sleeping pills, pain cream, cough medicine, allergy pills, Pepto-Bismol, Gravol, and so forth. Ignoring the mental and emotional costs of sickness (not to mention lost wages due to illness), the financial savings of a toxin-free home could easily surpass what your wife is spending on Young Living products.

> *Looking for a chemical free antiperspirant*
> *that actually works? Try a dab of YL*
> *Thieves Dentarome Ultra Toothpaste.*
> *Weird, but super-effective*

Yes, our oil shelf is full, but our medicine drawer is now practically empty (we keep tea in it now). My wife (tells me that she) usually spends one to three hundred dollars per month on oil products that help keep our family healthy. These products replace the expense of toxic products we no longer need and save us the costs of dealing with the negative effects of toxins.

If your concern is more with the business expense side of it, what are you comparing it to?

Not having a home-based business. Imagine you receive a letter from the government informing you of a new law mandating that every household must operate a home based business. Each year you are in violation of this law, the government will fine you $4000. Would you comply?

In essence, this law is already in effect. As stated by CPA Sandy Botkin (see Chapter 5), not having a home based business means you may be paying between 4,000 and $10,000 per year in avoidable taxes.

By not having a home-based business, you are probably down four grand.

Starting a new (non-MLM) business. Statistics show that the average cost of starting a service business is $18,000. Starting a retail business costs roughly $32,000. Monthly expenses vary, but

110

a minimum of $2000/month is reasonable (much more if you need to hire staff).

A non-MLM business will, therefore, cost you about $50,000/year.

Buying a Franchise. Depending on the type of franchise and if you will require significant overhead (building, vehicles, specialized equipment, etc.), most franchises will run you between $30,000 and $200,000 up front, plus ongoing expenses, royalties, and marketing fees.

Young Living Essential Oil business (rules and prices vary by country; the following are just estimates). To begin, your wife will have to buy an aptly named *starter kit* for about $200. After that, she will want to buy Young Living products for personal and family use; this will likely be about $150/month so she qualifies for all commissions and bonuses. Add to that, costs for samples, promotions, and other business expenses, which may add another $100/month. Training and personal development through regional meetings and national conventions will likely cost about $1000 and $2000 respectively for flights, accommodations, and food (I did not include these expenses for other businesses or franchises). Add all this up and her Young Living expenses will total approximately $6000/year.

Your wife will spend approximately $6000/year on her business. $1800 of that is for oils and other products that replace what you are buying already. Again, according to Botkin (Chapter 5), you will likely save at least $4000 in taxes. Based on these estimates, if she doesn't earn a penny, you will be out approximately $200 for the year.

Operating a Young Living business costs about $50,000 less than getting a traditional business or franchise up and running. Also, you are likely $3800 better off than you would be by doing nothing (and doing nothing tends to have very little upside potential).

Granted, having a home based business adds hassle (and no one hates hassle more than this guy), and maybe you're not sure if the financial benefit is worth it. If your wife really wants to use the oils and do the business, you may still be better off going with it. A look at your options explains why. You could,

1) Prevent your wife from having/continuing her YL business: Pay government $400/month and have a grumpy wife.
2) Support YL business: Pay $17/month (about 50 cents a day) to make your wife happy.

Remember incentives? It is like the government is saying, "Look, we both know what your wife is like when she doesn't get her way, and nobody wants that. How about we pay 400 bucks a month for you to keep her happy?"

Man, you are good to her!

If your concern is not so much about the money, but about the time, the next chapter is for you . . .

26. My Wife's Oil Business is taking time away from the Kids (and me)

Most guys who complain about the oils taking their wife away from the family are truly concerned about family time. Nevertheless, some guys – you know the type – are really just complaining because now they have to make more meals and look after the kids more than they are used to.

You know a husband is in the latter group when he has to look after his own kids for the evening and he calls it *babysitting*. Without asking you (or your wife) if this describes you, imagine the following scenario:

You and your wife both work outside the home. It is Friday afternoon and you are driving home from work, ready for the weekend. Your phone rings. You answer (hands free, of course). It is your wife.

"I have good news and I have bad news," she blurts out without even saying hello.

Sensing the seriousness in her tone, you quickly insist, "Bad news first," as you pull off the road and park in an empty lot and brace yourself for what she did to the car.

"I was laid off today," she said, surprisingly calm.

Your heart drops and you suddenly have a pain in the pit of your stomach. We need that money! How will we make all of our payments? We were having a tough time making ends meet as it was! Will we have to sell our house? We will have to cancel our vacation next month! You are feeling a bit dizzy and you are suddenly thankful you had parked.

All these thoughts happen in an instant. Then you suddenly realize something.

"You don't sound that upset about it," you comment.

She replies, "When my boss first told me, I was devastated. All I could think about was our bills and how we would lose our deposit on our vacation if we cancelled – which we will have to do. And retirement? What will I tell our kids? And my parents? And a hundred other things."

"Yeah," you say as you rub your forehead.

"But then my boss made me an offer," she added with a mysterious tone.

"What kind of offer?" You ask suspiciously.

"He said I could keep my job on one condition," she begins.

Before you could ask, she continues, "From Monday to Friday, I have to stay one hour longer and work. I also have to put in an hour of work on Saturdays. He said that I would not be paid for these extra hours. He also said that every hour must be productive and that I am not allowed to miss even one day. If I miss one day, I will lose my job. No being sick, no vacation, no excuses."

[Before finishing the story, just take a moment and reflect. How would you feel if this happened? Really, pause for a moment and consider how you would feel if your wife lost her job but then was given this offer . . .

. . . pause for reflection.

Okay, I will assume you have thought about how you would feel. Here is . . . *the rest of the story*:]

"I guess that is good news," you slowly reply, not at all convinced, "but . . ."

"No," your wife interrupts, "that is not the good news."

You begin to ask, "Well, wha . . ."

"Will you be quiet and listen?" your wife interjects, "Honestly, I am trying to . . ."

"Just tell me already!" you exclaim.

"The good news is that if I work one hour every day for free, after four years, I can quit my job and my boss will keep paying me my full salary for the rest of my life. I can retire on full salary after only four years! What do you think of that?" She shrieks.

You sit there, stunned. You don't know what to think. *Retire? In just four years? Full salary?*

Your wife interrupts your thoughts, "Now, there will have to be some sacrifices. With me working later every day, you will have to make some meals. You will have to be on kid duty more often. Oh, and we will have to cancel our vacation because I have a work conference I need to go to – and I can't miss it or the deal is off and I am fired. But, you guys could come with me and we could sightsee or swim in the pool in between sessions."

So, what would you think?

[Pause for reflection]

Are you thinking, *No way, I didn't get married and have kids just so I would have to stay home and look after them after work.*

Or, are you thinking, *One hour a day? Every day for four years? That will be an adjustment. Full salary pension in only four years?* "I'll pick up some pizza!"

Chances are, if you feel put out by your wife's business cutting into your leisure time, it is because you don't really believe she can earn good money at it. This becomes a self-fulfilling prophesy, if you make her feel guilty for working on her oil business, she probably won't devote much effort to it and even during the time she is working, she will be distracted and not very productive.

At the end of the day, if your wife feels guilty, she likely won't make much money, and she will quit (see Chapter 15). So, you can make her feel guilty until she quits and your life will remain much like it is right now, or, you can sacrifice an hour or so a day for a few years, encourage her, and help her succeed – and share in the wealth for the rest of your lives. It doesn't matter to me, which is easier for you?

27. What are the Odds that my Wife will make Money?

Can you believe, some guys actually ask what the odds are that their wives will make money building a Network Marketing/YL business? What a question! Hey, Poindexter! This isn't Vegas!

First, let me assure you, unless your wife also works at the mint, she will not *make* any money. Whatever money she acquires will not be made, it will be *earned*. While this may sound like foolish wordplay, it re-enforces a mindset. Your wife has to *earn* money.

What are the odds she will *earn* money? When you replace the word *make* with *earn*, the question doesn't even sound right, does it? I will try to answer it anyway.

Say you and 99 other people line up at the starting line of a marathon. What are the odds you will finish the race?

You can look at historical data to determine how many of these one hundred will actually finish the race. Let's say a dozen. What are the odds that one of those 12 is you?

It almost completely depends on you. Sure, a bus could blow through the police tape and take you out – that would not be your fault. But the more likely factors that affect your odds are within your control: How have you trained? Are your shoes on the wrong feet? Did you eat an entire pie the night before the race? Your wife's success in Network Marketing and with Young Living will almost entirely depend on your wife. This can be good news or it can be bad news.

Network Marketing is not "same for everyone" socialism. If your wife believes that everyone should get equal pay regardless of skills, effort, and results, then Network Marketing probably isn't for her. Obviously, she can still benefit from the products, but if she expects her business to grow without her persistent effort, she will likely be disappointed.

Here is where you can help your wife tremendously. Most people come from a background of being an employee. Maybe your wife has a job where seniority or politics – and not performance – are the top considerations for raises and promotions. Since she is likely doing her oil business part-time, she will be operating in two very different business realities and she will continually need to adjust her mindset accordingly.

According to the New York Daily News, approximately 70% of lottery winners are broke within seven years

Network Marketing is about owning and building your own *business*. Yes, a few people have made a lot of money with little effort on their part, but these are the rare exceptions. Incidentally, if making lots of money without working is your wife's business plan, forget Network Marketing and just buy lottery tickets – it is much less time consuming and you get to have fun scratching those little boxes.

There is an old saying in Network Marketing: *Treat it like a hobby and it will pay like a hobby; Treat it like a business and it will pay like a business.*

If your wife finds Young Living to be a fun hobby, that is fine. We have found that it is a great community with exceptional products and there are a lot worse things for her to spend money on. If, however, she considers herself a business builder, she will need to start thinking like an entrepreneur and get to work.

118

Additionally, if she does not treat Young Living like a business, kiss those tax benefits good-bye – the government doesn't subsidize hobbies.

So, back to the question: what are the odds she will earn money? If she avoids the trap of expecting other people to build her business, gets to work, learns the skills, takes advantage of tax breaks, puts in the effort, stays consistent, and remains persistent? The odds will be much greater than if she doesn't do any of these things. While you think about this, let's explore your alternatives.

If you and your wife keep doing what you have been doing (in your non-oil jobs), what are the odds you will succeed?

Statistics show that for every hundred people born in the US, 65 years later, *less than one* will be wealthy. Of these wealthy, nearly all will have obtained their wealth through inheritance or by owning their own business.

Of the 99 remaining seniors, about four will have enough saved up to retire while maintaining their current lifestyle.

Don't worry though, not all of the remaining 95 people will be anxious about money in retirement. Twenty-nine of them will be dead.

The remaining two-thirds of all 65 year olds will still be working or meagrely living on Social Security.

If financial success means retiring at 65 with enough savings to maintain the retiree's lifestyle, modern life has a 95% failure rate.

Maybe the question should not be about the odds of earning money in Network Marketing, but about the odds of you and your wife earning enough money with what you are doing now. I am not being insulting, I'm just a logical guy looking at statistics – these same numbers apply to me as much as they apply to you.

Speaking of statistics, wanna see how much people earn in their Young Living business? Of course you do . . .

28. What is the Income Potential?

Most guys want the bottom line, *how much will my wife earn with Young Living?*

[DISCLAIMER: If you have read the rest of this book, you know that a person's success in Network Marketing, Young Living, or any other business, depends on many factors – especially the knowledge, skills, and effort demonstrated by the individual. The following material is for informational and educational purposes only, and no promises or guarantees about the earnings of any specific person are implied.]

The Young Living Income Disclosure Statement can be found at https://www.youngliving.com/en_US/oppor tunity/income-disclosure

Many husbands are surprised to learn the income potential of a Young Living business. Yes, there are many women (and some men) earning a few hundred, or even a few thousand dollars a month pushing oils, and there are some doing even better than that. Much, much better.

This is a good place to review the Young Living *Income Disclosure Statement* (I.D.S.). All Network Marketing companies are required to provide an I.D.S. because they help protect prospective enrollees from being duped by exaggerated income claims. You can see a copy of Young Living's Income Disclosure Statement on the following page.

YOUNG LIVING 2016 U.S. INCOME DISCLOSURE STATEMENT

As a direct selling company selling essential oils, supplements, and other lifestyle products, Young Living offers opportunities for our members to build a business or simply receive discounts on our products.

Whatever your interest in the company, we hope to count you among the more than 2 million Young Living members joining us in our mission to bring Young Living essential oils to every home in the world.

What are my earning opportunities?

Members can earn commissions and bonuses as outlined in our Compensation Plan. As members move up in the ranks of Young Living, they become eligible for additional earning opportunities.

This document provides statistical, fiscal data about the average member income and information about achieving various ranks.

RANK	PERCENTAGE OF ALL MEMBERS[2]	MONTHLY INCOME[3]				ANNUALIZED AVERAGE INCOME[4]	MONTHS TO ACHIEVE THIS RANK[5]		
		Lowest	Highest	Median	Average		Low	Average	High
Distributor	94.0%	$0	$581	$0	$1	$12	N/A	N/A	N/A
Star	3.5%	$0	$811	$0	$77	$924	1	15	255
Senior Star	1.3%	$1	$5,557	$197	$240	$2,880	1	22	255
Executive	0.6%	$50	$12,139	$434	$514	$6,168	1	29	253
Silver	0.2%	$562	$25,546	$1,783	$2,227	$26,724	1	36	251
Gold	0.1%	$1,781	$46,820	$4,874	$6,067	$72,804	1	54	240
Platinum	<0.1%	$5,146	$85,993	$12,188	$15,324	$183,888	2	63	238
Diamond	<0.1%	$14,898	$140,333	$32,078	$39,566	$474,792	10	75	251
Crown Diamond	<0.1%	$37,227	$232,551	$64,256	$74,188	$990,256	14	83	236
Royal Crown Diamond	<0.1%	$58,392	$262,864	$155,248	$152,377	$1,828,524	17	106	230

The income statistics in this statement are for incomes earned by all active U.S. members in 2016. An "active" member is a member who made at least one product purchased in products in the previous 12 months. The average annual income for all members in this time was $25, and the median annual income for all members was $0. 51% of all members who enrolled in 2015 did not make a purchase with Young Living in 2016. 57% of all members who enrolled in 2014 did not continue with Young Living in 2016.

None that the compensation paid to members summarized in this disclosure do not include expenses incurred by a member in the operation or promotion of his or her business, which can vary widely and might include advertising or promotional expenses, product samples, training, rent, travel, telephone and Internet costs, and miscellaneous expenses. The earnings of the members in this chart are not necessarily representative of the income, if any, that a Young Living member can or will earn through the Young Living Compensation Plan. These figures should not be considered as guarantees or projections of your actual earnings or profits. Your success will depend on individual diligence, work, effort, sales skill, and market conditions. Young Living does not guarantee any income or rank success.

[1] Based on a count of all active members in 2016.
[2] Because a distributor's rank may change from during the year, these percentages are not based on individual distributor ranks during the entire year, but based on the average distribution of distributor ranks during the entire year.
[3] Because a distributor's rank may change from during the year, these incomes are not based on individual distributor incomes throughout the entire year, but based on earnings of all distributors qualifying for each rank during any month throughout the year.
[4] This is calculated by multiplying the average monthly incomes by 12.
[5] These statistics include all historical earnings data for each rank and is not limited to people who achieved these ranks in 2016.
[6] Members who do not make at least one product purchase in the previous 12-months have their membership terminated.

YOUNG LIVING
ESSENTIAL OILS

Because of their design, Income Disclosure Statements may paint an overly negative picture for those thinking about building a Network Marketing business. To demonstrate, here are figures taken from the Young Living I.D.S.:

Rank	Percent of Members	Average Monthly Income	Number of Months to Reach Rank
Distributor	94.0%	$1	N/A
Star	3.5%	$77	15
Senior Star	1.3%	$240	22
Executive	0.6%	$514	29
Silver	0.2%	$2,227	36
Gold	0.1%	$6,067	54
Platinum	<0.1%	$15, 324	63
Diamond	<0.1%	$39,566	75
Crown Diamond	<0.1%	$74,188	83
Royal Crown Diamond	<0.1%	$152,377	106

What does this table show you?

First, Young Living classifies most enrollees as Distributors, and most Distributors earn practically nothing.

It also (kind of) answers your question, *how much will my wife earn in her Young Living business?* Her average monthly income will almost certainly be somewhere between $1 and $152,000. Not very helpful. Let's look closer and see if we can get a little better idea . . .

Notice the average time it takes to reach each rank? 36 months for Silver, 75 months for Diamond? Why does it say N/A (Not Applicable) for Distributor?

People who want oils can do one of two things: they can buy retail, or they can sign up for a free membership and immediately get a 24% discount on products. If they decide to buy retail, they are not members, they do not get a discount, and they are not eligible to earn any money. They are, therefore, not included in the I.D.S.

If a customer chooses to become a member, however, they qualify for the product discounts and may earn commissions and bonuses. Because they are now *eligible* to earn payments, they are *automatically* included as a Distributor on the Income Disclosure Statement. This instant inclusion explains why it takes no time to become a Distributor. Automatically including all wholesale customers as Distributors can be problematic when attempting to determine what an active business builder can earn.

There is no way of knowing why a person signed up for the free membership. She may have wanted to start a Young Living business or she may have just wanted a discount on her oils. In my experience, most people listed as Distributers just wanted the oils as I know no one who tried to build a business that did not at least reach the rank of Star.

Based on my observations, the 94% listed as Distributors likely did not even attempt to business build. If we remove these *customers* from the Income Disclosure Statement, that leaves us with the percentages of *business builders* who achieved each rank (even though not all people who reach ranks actually tried to build a business, but again, being conservative):

Rank	Percent of Members*	Average Monthly Income	Number of Months to Reach Rank
Star	58.0%	$77	15
Senior Star	21.5%	$240	22
Executive	10.0%	$514	29
Silver	3.5%	$2,227	36
Gold	1.5%	$6,067	54
Platinum	<1.5%	$15, 324	63
Diamond	<1.5%	$39,566	75
Crown Diamond	<1.5%	$74,188	83
Royal Crown Diamond	<1.5%	$152,377	106

*Rounded to nearest .5

Take from this what you want, the Income Disclosure Statement shows there is wide variety of outcomes, but if your wife actually works at building her Young Living business for three to five years, $5,000/month is a reasonable goal.

[Again, the above charts are for informational purposes only and no income guarantee is being made. Results vary. For more information about the Network Marketing opportunity and to read some real life examples of people who have succeeded in YL, check out *The Four Year Career, Young Living Edition*, by Richard Bliss Brooke. Warning: It will inspire you.]

More evidence that this is not a pyramid scheme

Before moving on, do you see how the Income Disclosure Statement demonstrates why Young Living is not a pyramid scheme?

As mentioned earlier, the I.D.S. does not differentiate between those who just wanted to be a wholesale customer (and earn nothing) and those who tried to build a business (but earned nothing).

Remember earlier in the book when I mentioned the criteria for determining whether or not a business was a pyramid scheme? What was the primary deciding factor?

[Play *Final Jeopardy* music in your head]

Was the money exchanged for legitimate products or services?

The Income Disclosure Statement indicates that most people are only interested in Young Living as a supplier of their essential oil products, and *not* as a business opportunity. Most people are merely consumers with no apparent interest in recruiting, sponsoring, or building a business. A company that did not have a legitimate product or service would have few customers and many recruiters. Young Living is just the opposite, many customers and relatively few recruiters.

Earlier I mentioned how I have a Customer Loyalty Membership Card from my local gas station. I go there, buy gas, and get a discount. That's all I want – a discount on my gas. If the company never sends me a cheque, would I ever claim that they swindled me out of the money I spent on gas?

What if I buy a bike and no longer need to buy gas? Was I ripped off because I spent hundreds of dollars buying gas at that gas station last year when I did have a car? These things don't even make sense – I didn't *lose money*, I bought gas!

Most of the people represented on the Income Disclosure Statement just wanted to buy oils at wholesale prices. No one swindled them and they did not fail at Network Marketing, *they just wanted oils!*

I must point out the irony that the same people who accuse Network Marketing of being a pyramid scheme also point to Income Disclosure Statements like Young Living's as proof that Network Marketing doesn't work (because so few make money). The facts that most people are just customers (not recruiters), and do not even try to make money, prove it is NOT a pyramid scheme!

Breathe Joel . . .

29. *I don't want to Live off my Wife* and other Hang-ups.

For various reasons, some husbands are uncomfortable with the thought of their wife building a successful Young Living (or any other) Network Marketing business. Some of the most common reasons are:

- Perception from friends and family that Network Marketing is not a legitimate business.
- Pride/cultural expectation that the husband should be the (primary) bread winner.
- Feelings of losing masculinity if the wife is the money earner. This can be worse if the husband begins taking over more and more household duties.
- Money can equal power. If a wife starts earning five, ten, or fifteen thousand dollars a month, it may affect the relationship dynamic.
- The husband is afraid of becoming a trophy husband. He envisions himself going to her conventions; while she hobnobs with the million dollar earners, he just smiles and makes awkward small talk with the other tag-along husbands. Hey Snowflake, if you find yourself in this position, avoid eye contact by pretending to look for something in your man purse.

The truth is, at some point, most Network Marketing husbands feel some or all of these sentiments.

When the business is new, the fledgling entrepreneur will be unsure about herself and the business, and more money may be going out than coming in. At this point, her husband may be concerned about what people think. Instead of admitting he is embarrassed, he covers his pride by complaining about having to do laundry (plus, doing laundry sucks almost as much as cross country skiing).

If the wife sticks it out and the money starts rolling in, however, most of the husbands who have been "retired" by their wives are more than happy to quit their jobs and live off their sugar mommas – even if that means washing their own underwear from time to time.

Paying your kids to do housework may be
a home-business write-off

May I let you in on a little secret? The window of time when you will have to do laundry (cooking, cleaning, etc.) may be relatively short. At first, your wife will have time for most of these chores. As her business grows, she will get busier, and you may become well acquainted with the household appliances. Before long, however, the hope is that she will be making enough money to hire someone to do laundry and clean . . . then you can come up to Saskatchewan and you and me will go fishin' for some of them Northern Pike!

The concerns listed above (and others) are legitimate feelings you may have. One way to overcome most of these concerns is to try to find ways to make the business a partnership rather than just her gig. This may mean that while she makes calls you make supper. Or, if you are so inclined, help her with some of the non-oil aspects of the business like technical (computer) or tax support. This way success becomes a team effort (plus, if you do her taxes, you know *exactly* how much she spent on oils).

Ultimately, it comes down to your retirement choices outlined in Chapter 13. You can work your jobs for 40 years and try to save a million or two bucks for retirement, or, you can get over your hang-ups, do some laundry while she builds a business, and reap the rewards for the rest of your life. Send me an email to tell me which option you prefer – I'll reply when I finish unloading the dishwasher.

30. Parting Words

Well, you made it! You read every word of the book, line by line, and cover to cover. You honoured your wife by fulfilling her request – you read this book simply because she asked you to and you love her. You are awesome!

Feeling guilty for just skipping to the end yet?

Don't worry, I have you covered for the exam (your wife grilling you), here are some cheat notes:

1) Network Marketing is being paid to share products you like with friends. Compensation plans involve the familiar practices of a loyalty program, referral bonuses, and commission sales.

2) Network Marketing is huge in both sales volume and number of people involved.

3) For tax reasons, everyone should consider having a home-based business.

4) Network Marketing is nothing like a Ponzi scheme.

5) Network Marketing businesses operate on a pyramid structure. So does the global economy, the United States, Fortune 500 companies, and nearly every other business. Organic growth is also in the shape of a pyramid.

6) About one in 400 Network Marketing companies have been illegal pyramid schemes that have been shut down because they focussed on recruiting rather than product sales.

7) Network Marketing allows you freedom to control your destiny because, unlike most businesses, your rank and pay are determined by how far you are from the bottom, not by how close you are to the top.

8) There are ways to share the products and opportunity without alienating friends and family – your wife should learn these skills.

9) Passive income is the key to freedom and wealth.

10) Few people fail at Network Marketing, but many quit.

11) Historically, there have been legit snake oils that work, and counterfeit snake oils that don't; essential oils are the same – get the good ones.

12) In spite of evidence that essential oils enhance health, doctors rarely endorse them because they are not FDA (or Health Canada) approved drugs. Essential oils are not medicine, and Doctors practice medicine.

13) Be careful with peppermint around the eyes. 'Nuff said.

14) Building a significant Network Marketing business is a mid to long-term game (*at least* three consistent years). Like all new ventures, at first your wife will work harder than for what she is paid, then – if she persists – the reverse will be true. She has to be patient and learn how to build a business.

15) Of the people who *actively pursue* Network Marketing as a business, most earn a little money, some earn significant money, and a few earn BIG money.

Well, that's good for now. I wish you health and wealth in whatever endeavors you and your wife embark upon in your journey together. Now, get back to watching NASCAR!

All the best,

Joel

Disclaimer

Statements in this book have not been evaluated by the Food and Drug Administration or Health Canada. Information in this book is for educational purposes only and not intended to diagnose, treat, cure, or prevent any disease. For health concerns, always consult with a qualified healthcare professional.

Additionally, no specific legal, tax, or income claims are made or implied in this book. Individual results in Network Marketing vary greatly. Information and examples provided are for educational purposes only. Always consult a professional for legal, tax, or financial planning advice.

About the Author

Between 2012 and 2015, Joel received his B.Ed, M.Ed, B.A. (Economics), and PhD degrees from the University of Saskatchewan where his peers quickly recognized his talents and insights as an author and a teacher. Portions of his thesis became required reading in undergrad and graduate studies courses in the College of Education. During this time, Joel also joined the Faculty of Education as a professor. His career has also included time as a school teacher and principal.

Joel has a passion for teaching and empowering others through the sharing of knowledge. He believes that people should not be told what to think, but they should be given the appropriate information so they can make informed decisions for themselves.

Joel's wife, Shari, is building a thriving Young Living business in Saskatoon, Saskatchewan, Canada, where they live with their four children. Besides being a business and athletic coach, Joel is an avid sports fan and fisherman.

Contact Joel at: *forthehusbandbook@gmail.com*

Made in the USA
San Bernardino, CA
05 December 2018